Leading Strategy of the Prophet [PBUH]

Prof Javed Iqbal Saani, PhD

PhD, MBA (MIS), MBA (Finance), BBA

Intellectual Capital Enterprise Limited, London

Copyright © 2018 Prof Javed Iqbal Saani

All rights reserved.

No reproduction of the book in any form such as electronic, photocopying, scanning, recording or otherwise. It also includes storing for retrieval purposes or transmitting through electronic media i.e. email. Prior written permission of the publisher may require doing any of the above under the relevant act that follows the Copyright, Design, and Patent Act 1988.

Authors and the publisher are not responsible for any damage caused by the application/use of the concepts, techniques, instruction, or actions. The authors and the publisher refuse any implied warranties or related matters.

ISBN 9781727090192

Published by Intellectual Capital Enterprise Limited
ICE Kemp House, 152-160 City Road
London, EC1 V2N
Printed in England

CONTENTS

About the author vii
Dedication xv
Acknowledgement xvii
Preface xix

1 INTRODUCTION TO LEADING 1
   Introduction 1
   Motivation 2
      Monetary incentives 8
   Motivation through respecting people 11
   Leadership 16
   Influencing power 18
   Relationship management or Management by relations 20
   Role Model 22
   Accountability 23
   Establishment of Justice 24
   Consultation and involvement 24

2 SOCIAL RESPONSIBILITY 27
   Introduction 27

Individual measures 28

Collective measures 30

3 PROPHET (ﷺ) AS AN INNOVATOR 33

Introduction 33

The economic innovation 37

Entering the foreign markets 38

4 MANAGERIAL STRATEGIES 41

Introduction 41

Pro-active management style 42

Innovative solution of problems 44

5 FINANCIAL MANAGEMENT 49

Introduction 49

Sources of finance 50

Areas of spending 51

Circulation of wealth 53

6 DECISION MAKING 57

Introduction 57

Identifying and choosing alternatives 58

Structured and unstructured decision 59

Decision rules 60

Prophet's way of making decisions 60

Group decisions 62

Long term and short-term decisions 63

    The speciality of prophet's decisions 64

7 CULTURAL CHANGE 67

    Introduction 67

    Change in belief 69

    Mutual respect 69

    Promote greeting 70

    Obeying manager/boss 70

    Offering good advice 72

    Supporting subordinates 74

    Merit based Selection and recruitment 76

    Learning organisation 77

    Role model 78

    Managing issues 79

    Ethics 82

    Organisation policy 83

    Other Values 84

    Quality management 86

    Showing by doing 86

8 CASE STUDY: THE TREATY OF HODHABIA 89

    Introduction 89

    The story 89

    Managerial Implications 93

Bibliography 99

Index 105
Other books by the author (s) 109
Notes 119

About the author

Javed Iqbal was brought up in Rawalakot (AJ&K). He received his Ph.D. from the University of Salford and an MBA (Information Management) from the University of Hull. Previously Dr. Iqbal received BBA and an MBA (in Finance) from the University of AJ&K both with distinction.

Professor Iqbal joined Iqra University Islamabad campus as an associate professor in 2006. He became the head of Department of Technology Management in International Islamic University Islamabad (IIUI) in 2012. Dr. Iqbal joined AKU (AJ&K) as a professor in 2015 and has been appointed as a Dean Faculty of  Management Sciences. He is associated with London School of Commerce (LSC) these days. His article titled "Learning from a Doctoral Research Project: Structure and Content of a Research Proposal" has been ranked by the Deakin University of Australia as the best piece of research for doctoral students. This research paper is widely used and referred all over the world. Dr. Javed Iqbal has been nominated by an international organization for the Award of Distinguished Scientist for his research contribution. Professor Iqbal has published 22 research articles and 25 books so far. He has developed an interest in Islamic Leadership Style recently. Professor Iqbal has published in such International Journals as *Electronic Journal of Business Research Methods*, *European Journal of Social Sciences*, *Œconomica*, and *European Journal of Scientific Research*. His books on various subjects are available on Amazon, details are at the end of the book.

Say (to them, O Muhammad): Are those who know equal with those who know not? But only men of understanding will pay heed. [Az-Zumar: 9]

Anas (May Allah be pleased with him) reported:
The Messenger of Allah (ﷺ) said, "He who goes forth in search of knowledge is considered as struggling in the Cause of Allah until he returns." [At- Tirmidhi].

Abu'd-Darda' (RA) said, "I heard the Messenger of Allah, may Allah bless him and grant him peace, say,

1. 'Allah will make the path to the Garden easy for anyone who travels a path in search of knowledge.

2. Angels spread their wings for the seeker of knowledge out of pleasure for what he is doing.

3. Everyone in the heavens and everyone in the earth asks forgiveness for a man of knowledge, even the fish in the water.

4. The superiority of the man of knowledge to the man of worship is like the superiority of the moon to all the planets.

5. The men of knowledge are the heirs of the Prophets.

6. The Prophets bequeath neither dinar nor dirham; they bequeath knowledge. Whoever takes it has taken an ample portion.'"

[Abu Dawud and at-Tirmidhi; Riyadh us Salihin, Hadith 1388, p. 211]

It was by the mercy of God that you were lenient with them (O Muhammad), for if you had been severe and hard-hearted, they would have forsaken you. So, pardon them and ask (God's) forgiveness for them and consult with them upon the conduct of affairs. [Al-e-Imran: 159]

Hadhrat Ibn 'Umar (Radhiyallao anho) reports that Rasulullaah (Sallallaho alaihe wasallam) said "Three persons are such as will have no fear of the horrors of the Day of Judgement, nor they will be required to render any account. They will stroll merrily on mounds of musk until the people are relieved of rendering their account. One is a person who learnt the Qur'an, merely seeking Allah's pleasure and therewith leads people in salaat in a manner that they are pleased with him; the second person is the one who invites men to salaat for the pleasure of Allah alone. <u>The third person is the one who has fair dealings between him and his master, as well as between himself and his subordinates</u>" [Quoted by Al-Tibrani in Al-Majam Al-Slaasa; Fazail-e-Amaal, Virtues of the Holy Qur'an, Hadith 36]

'Abdullah ibne-'Umar Radiyallahu 'anhuma narrates that a person came to Nabi and asked: O Rasulullah (ﷺ)! How many times may I forgive my servant? Nabi remained silent. The man asked again: O Rasulullah (ﷺ)! How many times may I forgive my servant? He replied: Everyday seventy times. (Tirmidhi) Note: In Arabic, the figure 'seventy' is used to express too many in number. [Muntakhib Ahadith, p. 415]

Dedication

To my parents who invested heavily for our education and remained engaged in prayers for our success and good being

Acknowledgement

Special gratitude is due to all those who helped me to compile the work. I am also obliged to my family who spared me to embark on the project. They also provide valuable information which enriched the contents of this effort. May Allah reward them for their contribution? Ameen!

Preface

All prayers to Allah, the exalted, slat wa slam to all the prophets (AS) especially upon the last (ﷺ), mercy and blessings upon his noble companions. May Allah (SWT) bestow upon his forgiveness to the entire ummah and ummah of all the prophets (AS). And all those who received the right guidance.

Since long I was working on the topic, but the work was getting delayed with one or the other reasons. Finally, with the help of Allah, the exalted the projects ended. The purpose of the book was to identify the leadership qualities of the beloved prophet (ﷺ) in contemporary language. Management as an independent filed of knowledge emerged in the last century when "The Principles of Scientific Management" was published in 1911. The world started to believe that the field of management was invented; the field was in practice since the birth of the second human being on the surface of the earth. We understand that she was our grandmother Hawwa [Eve] (AS). Her existence was the reason of the first family i.e. an organisation. The holy Qur'an describes that male is the head of this organisation because Allah, the exalted, has appointed him. And male also spends money on women at the time of marriage and afterwards. It suggests that the management emerged on the day Adham (AS) was appointed as the manager of his family unit.

As we believe our prophet (ﷺ) was appointed as the last prophet (ﷺ) and a set of guidance was given to him to manage the affairs of people and the state of Madinah. He (ﷺ) had managed the organisation effectively and efficiently. This book is an attempt to describe his way of management focusing on "Leading" aspect. Two books about planning and organising function of the prophet (ﷺ) were already published. It is the third one and hopefully, the final would emerge soon about "Controlling".

The book contains 8 chapters. Seven of them are dealing with various aspects of leadership. The first one discusses generic topics about the subject such as motivation and leading strategy etc. Management writers describe other topics sometimes under the "Leadership" function and sometime as an independent topic. For instance, social responsibility or fiscal management. However, they are related with the leadership viewpoint; I have included them with this in perspective.

It is not an exhausted treatise on the topic it is the humble beginning. Keen researchers can do more work on the subject.

There are many books and articles about the topic or a part of it. For instance, the prophet (ﷺ) as a military leader etc. However, the present work has been compiled from the management perspective. Therefore, topics have been arranged accordingly.

I pray to Allah, the exalted, to accept the humble effort and make it a source of forgiveness for me and the entire ummah. It may be a source of guidance for readers. Ameen!

Suggestions are welcome so that they may be incorporated in the future editions.

Prof Javed Iqbal Saani, Ph. D

Manchester September 3, 2018

1 INTRODUCTION TO LEADING

Introduction

A manager/leader is the one who offers support to subordinates, keeping them motivated, providing them required resources and resolving their issues arising out of work or beyond. A leader must know what work followers are doing, can do himself and able to monitor it. Given that let us look at some of the examples from the life of the prophet (ﷺ) regarding these matters.

If we assume family as an organizational unit (and it is not an illogical assumption because Allah (SWT) has commenced the world with this unit) than his family life informed us that he used to do his own jobs and he used to help his wives in the day-to-day household matters. At the occasion of war of trench, he participated for digging the trench himself.[1]

---

[1] Mubarikpuri, p. 413.

When we examine the organisational life of the prophet (ﷺ) a rich picture of his management style emerged. Salient features of his managerial approach included motivation, leadership, team management, and communication.[1] We debate these topics in connection with the life of the prophet (ﷺ) to understand the subject from his perspective.

Motivation

He was constantly motivating his companions; when sahabah (RA) were sustaining oppression from the infidels, he motivates them by saying: be patient, your reward is paradise.

It may be worthwhile to mention that the prophetic strategy of motivation was based upon the reward in the world and in the Hereafter. However, he also applied other motivational strategies. The companions were persecuted in Makkah so they required motivation to remain steadfast on their religion. The story of Yasir (RA) was a distinguished incident because his wife Summaya (RA) was martyred during brutalities. Hazrat Shaikh Zakerya writes,

Hadhrat Ammaar (RA) and his parents were also subjected to the severest afflictions. They were

---

[1] Dyck and Neubert, 2009, p. xiii-xv. These authors described these topics in various chapters. Each chapter discuses one element at a time.

tormented on the scorching sands of Makkah. Nabi (Sallallahu Alayhi Wasallam) while passing by <u>them would ask them to be patient, giving them glad tidings about Jannat</u>. Ammaar's father Yasir (RA) died after prolonged suffering at the hands of the persecutors. His mother Sumayya (RA) was killed by Abu Jahl, who put his spear through the most private part of her body, causing her death. She had refused to leave Islam despite terrible torture in her old age. The blessed lady was the first to meet shahaadat in the cause of Islam. The first masjid in Islam was built by Ammaar (RA).

Allah (SWT) the prophet (ﷺ) and the companions, in general, to respond against any aggression. The only way was to remain tolerant. However, there ought to be a motivator. And that was the goodness of the life in the Hereafter. The prophet (ﷺ) offered two blessings: the pleasure of Allah (SWT) and the entry in the paradise. The prophet (ﷺ) was promising it and the companions believed it and made a sacrifice for it.

In connection with the possessions and luxurious lifestyle Umer (RA) once visited the prophet (ﷺ) and reported the following conversation with the prophet (ﷺ).

I noticed that the contents of his room consisted of only three pieces of skin and a handful of barley lying in a corner. I looked about, but I failed to find anything else. I began to weep.

He asked; 'Why are you weeping?' I replied: 'O, Nabi of Allah! Why should I not weep? I can see the imprint of the mat's pattern on your body, and I have also noticed all your belongings that you have in this room. O, Nabi of Allah! Make dua that Allah Ta'ala may grant ample provisions for us.

The Persians and the Romans who have no true faith and do not worship Allah Ta'ala but worship their kings, the Caesar and Chosroes, presently live in gardens with streams running in their midst, but the chosen Nabi and the accepted slave of Allah Ta'ala live in such dire poverty!' Nabi (Sallallahu Alayhi Wasallam) was resting against his pillow, but when he heard me talk like this, he sat up and said, 'O, 'Umar! Are you still in doubt about this matter? Ease and comfort in the Hereafter are much better than ease and comfort in this world.

The disbelievers are enjoying their share of the good things in this very world, whereas we have all such things in store for us in the next. I begged him: 'O, Nabi of Allah! Ask forgiveness for me. I was really in the wrong."[1]

---

[1] Kandhelvi, Zakerya, M, Fazaial-e-Amaal, p. 61.

Hazrat Shaikh comments on the above, he writes, "Look at the household possessions of the ruler in this world and in the hereafter, the beloved Nabi of Allah Ta'ala. See how he rebukes 'Umar (RA) when he asks him to make dua (supplication) for some relief and comfort in this world." (p. 40) The prophet (ﷺ) once again directed the attention of Umer (RA) towards the life in the Hereafter. However, the prophet (ﷺ) also offered the success of this life upon acceptance of Islam and adoption of righteous lifestyle.

The prophet (ﷺ) also persuaded Quraysh while invited them towards Islam. Moulana Noamani states about it. The prophet (ﷺ) summoned Quraysh on Safa hill and presented Islam to them, but they did not care. He asked Ali (RA) to cook food for them a few days later. The prophet (ﷺ) invited the entire family of Abdul Muttalib, in fact, it was a good occasion for a demonstration of his religion. The prophet (ﷺ) said following food, "I have brought the religion which is enough for this world and the Hereafter. Who was ready to share the responsibility with me?" No one responded except Ali (RA). He stood up and said, I am ready to support yourself despite many limitations.

One of the illustrious incidents in the history of Islam was the migration of the prophet (ﷺ) to Madinah. He was accompanied with Abu Bakr (RA) in the expedition, Molan Yusaf Kandehvi writes at this occasion,

Under the veil of the night, Rasulullaah (ﷺ) and Hadhrat Abu Bakr (RA) left for the cave in the Thowr mountain, which is mentioned in the Quraan. Hadhrat Ali bin Abi Taalib (RA) slept on Rasulullaah's (ﷺ) bed so that Rasulullaah (ﷺ) could hide from Mushrikeen spies (who would think that Rasulullaah (ﷺ) is asleep in the house). The Mushrikeen spend the night walking about and discussing how they would leap on to the person sleeping and tie him up. They continued in this manner until dawn broke and they saw Hadhrat Ali (RA) stand up from Rasulullaah (ﷺ) bed. When they asked Hadhrat Ali (RA) where Rasulullaah (ﷺ) was, he said that he did not know. They then realised that Rasulullaah (ﷺ) had left Makkah. The Mushrikeen then took to their mounts and started searching for Rasulullaah. (ﷺ). They also sent messages to the people at the various oases, instructing them to capture Rasulullaah (ﷺ) and promising them large rewards. They reached the cave of ~h6wr where Rasulullaah (ﷺ) and Hadhrat Abu Bakr (RA) hid and had even climbed on top of the cave (where the entrance was). Rasulullaah (ﷺ) heard their voices and Hadhrat Abu Bakr (RA) became worried and frightened. Rasulullaah (ﷺ) then said to him.

"Do not grieve (do not fear for my safety). Verily Allaah is with us (and He will protect us from the Kuffaar)." {Surah Taubah, verse 40) Rasulullaah

(ﷺ) then made du'aa to Allaah and Allaah sent peace and tranquillity to them.

Look at the event from different perspectives. The noble team had arrived in the cave from under the swards. The enemies were still following them to fulfil their long-lasting desire to eliminate the lamp of guidance. The team had to continue travel towards the new destination. The danger of enemy did exist. However, should they leave safely, they could reach the safe heaven. The prophet (ﷺ) corroborated the fear of Abu Bakr (RA). The prophet (ﷺ) said with confidence, "...Do not grieve (do not fear for my safety). Verily Allah is with us (and He will protect us from the Kuffaar) ..." {Surah Taubah: 40). Not only that the prophet (ﷺ) raised his hands towards Allah for his help. Allah had bestowed His blessing and mercy as described here.

> So, Allah caused His tranquillity (serenity, mercy, and peace) to descend on him, assisted him with an army (of angels and other creation) that you had not seen. And (Allah) placed the word of the Kuffaar (the call to Shirk) at the very bottom while the word of Allaah (the Kalimah) is right at the top. Allaah is Mighty, The Wise. (Surah Taubah: 40)

The prophet's (ﷺ) actions removed the fears of Abu Bakr (RA). We can infer that it enhanced the motivation of his companion which implies that it became an example for Muslims to follow in the tough time. Remember that a few good words from a manger encourage more than heaps of money and fringe benefits organisations offered today. Management experts experimented it in the late 1920s [1] to understand what the prophet (ﷺ) practiced centuries ago.

Monetary incentives

The prophet (ﷺ) had adopted a welfare strategy for the monetary benefits of his followers. There were three types of employees at that time: slaves, soldiers, and government officials.

People used to buy slaves for a lump sum. Slaves were poor people, unable to pay money to get freedom. Most important monetary favour for them to get freedom in exchange for the sum the owner was asking. The prophet's (ﷺ) right-hand Abu Bakr (RA) was a wealthy businessman. He paid the heavy amount for the freedom of Bilal (RA), Amir bin Faheerah (RA), Labinah (RA), Zanarah (RA), Nahdia (RA) and Um-e-Abees (RA). We have already seen in the above paragraphs that the prophet (ﷺ) was

---

[1] Mayo E. (1933) The Human Problems of an Industrial Civilization. Harvard University Press.

ready to free Zaid bin Harsa (RA) free of cost provided he wanted to join his family.

The soldiers were the second type of people working for the prophet (ﷺ) and for the Islamic state of Madinah. They were a volunteer. There was a tribal system prior to Islam in the Arab peninsula (in general) where the defence was the responsibility of the whole Trible in case of any security issue with other tribes etc. Member of a tribe used to train himself to operate the prevalent weapons for the purpose. Therefore, there were no regular military expenditures. The prophet (ﷺ) used to collect working capital prior to any armed encounter. However, the prophet (ﷺ) used to distribute the spoils of war to the participants. It was a monetary reward.

The third type of employees were the government officials. For instance, the people employed for the collection of zakah. Allah (SWT) ordained to pay remuneration to the collectors. The holy Quran states,

> Zakah expenditures are only for the poor and for the needy and for those employed for it and for bringing hearts together [for Islam] and for freeing captives [or slaves] and for those in debt and for the cause of Allah and for the [stranded] traveller –an obligation [imposed] by Allah. And Allah is Knowing and Wise. (Al-Taubah: 60)

In addition to the monetary benefit, Islam offers the rewards in the Hereafter. Both function as a motivator. The prophet (ﷺ) had augmented these with humanistic aspects of making people happy and willing to work with him.

The verbal motivation was part of his strategy. Look at this aspect of his life.

Abu Hurairah (May Allah be pleased with him) reported: We were sitting in the company of the Messenger of Allah (ﷺ), and Abu Bakr and `Umar (May Allah be pleased with them) were also present. Suddenly, the Messenger of Allah (ﷺ) got up and left us. When he was late to return to us, we began to worry lest he should meet with trouble in our absence. I was the first to be alarmed and set out in search of him until I came to a garden belonging to Banu-Najjar (a section of the Ansar). I went around it is looking for an entrance but failed to find one. However, I saw a stream of water flowing into the garden from a well outside. I drew myself together like a fox and slinked into the place and reached the Messenger of Allah (ﷺ). He said, "Is it Abu Hurairah?" I replied in the affirmative. He asked, "What is the matter with you?" I replied, "You were sitting with us and then you left us and delayed for a time. Fearing you had met with some adversities we got alarmed. I was the first to be alarmed. So, when I came to this garden, I squeezed myself like a fox and these people are coming behind me." He (the Prophet (ﷺ)) gave me his sandals and said, "O Abu Hurairah! Take these sandals of mine, and whoever you meet outside this garden testifying that La ilaha illallah (There is no true god except Allah), be assured of it in his heart, give him the glad tidings that he will enter Jannah." (Abu Hurairah then narrated the Hadith in full). [Muslim, Riyadus-Saliheen, Hadith Number 710]

Although the quotation is about the life the Hereafter but is equally applicable here. Those would be successful who would have done good actions (or earned satisfactory performance) while living in this world. The glad tiding for them.

It shows the strategy of the prophet (ﷺ) to motivate his followers, employees, and the public.

Motivation through respecting people

It is important to understand that employees or people working with someone are human beings. They like *cordial treatment* from their seniors and colleagues. The prophet (ﷺ) had demonstrated it in many ways. For example, he used to visit his sick companions. Look at this small story.

Narrated Ibn `Abbas: Allah's Messenger (ﷺ) entered upon sick man to pay him a visit, and said to him, "Don't worry, Allah willing, (your sickness will be) an expiation for your sins." The man said, "No, it is but a fever that is boiling within an old man and will send him to his grave." On that, the Prophet (ﷺ) said, "Then yes, it is so." [Sahih al-Bukhari 5662; In-book reference: Book 75, Hadith 23; USC-MSA web (English) reference: Vol. 7, Book 70, Hadith 566]

The prophet (ﷺ) further elaborated the act of visiting sick in the following words.

Thuwair [and he is Ibn Abi Fakhitah] narrated that: His father said: "Ali took me by the hand and said: 'Come with us to pay a visit to Al-Hasan.' So, we found that Abu Musa was with him.' Ali - peace be upon him - said: 'O Abu Musa! Did you come to visit (the sick) or merely (stop by to) visit?' He said: 'No, to visit (the sick).' So, Ali said: 'I heard the Messenger of Allah saying: "No Muslim visits (the sick) Muslims in the morning, except that seventy-thousand angels, sent Salat upon him until the evening, and he does not visit at night except that seventy thousand angels sent Salat upon him until the morning, and there will be a garden for him in Paradise."

[Jami` at-Tirmidhi 969; In-book reference: Book 10, Hadith 5; English translation: Vol. 2, Book 5, Hadith 969]

Another motivational strategy of the prophet (ﷺ) was to *encourage* his companions to do something. Molana Kandhelvi narrates a story regarding it.

Rasulullaah (ﷺ) Gives Encouragement before a Battle and the Statement of Hadhrat Umayr bin Hamaam.

Hadhrat Anas (RA) says, "Rasulullaah sent Basbas (RA) to spy on what the caravan of Abu Sufyaan was doing. 'When he reported back to Rasulullaah (ﷺ), there was none with him in the room besides me." The narrator says that Hadhrat Anas (RA) also mentioned the names of some wives of Rasulullaah (ﷺ) (who were in the room), but he (the narrator) does not remember who they were. After Hadhrat Basbas (RA) had informed Rasulullaah (ﷺ) about the news, Rasulullaah (ﷺ) left the house and announced, "We are leaving in pursuit (of the caravan). Whoever has his mount present should ride with us." When some Sahabah (RA) requested permission to fetch their animals that were in the upper part of Madinah, Rasulullaah (ﷺ) said, "No. Only those whose mounts are present may ride." Rasulullaah (ﷺ) and the Sahabah (RA) rod off and arrived at Badr before the Mushrikeen. When the Mushrikeen arrived, Rasulullaah said to the Sahabah (RA) one of you should do anything until I act." When the Mushrikeen came close, Rasulullaah (ﷺ) said, "Stand up and advance to a Jannah that is as wide as the heavens and the earth!" Hadhrat Umayr bin Hamaam (RA) from the Ansaar asked, "O Rasulullaah (ﷺ) A Jannah that is as wide as the heavens and the earth?" "Certainly," confirmed Rasulullaah (ﷺ). Hadhrat Umayr (RA) exclaimed, "Wow!" When Rasulullaah (ﷺ) asked him why he said this, Hadhrat Umayr (RA) replied, "O Rasulullaah (ﷺ)By Allaah! There is no reason other than that I should be among its inhabitants." Rasulullaah (ﷺ) assured him, "You are certainly from amongst its inhabitants." Hadhrat Umayr (RA) took out some dates from his quiver and started eating them. However, he then said, "If I live until I have eaten these dates, it will take too much time." He then threw down the dates he had left and jumped into the thick of battle until he was martyred. May Allaah shower His mercy on him. Ibn Is'haaq narrates that Rasulullaah (ﷺ) went to the Sahabah (RA) to give them encouragement saying, "I swear by the Being Who controls the life of Muhammad! Allaah shall enter Jannah every man who fights the Mushrikeen today and is martyred while he is patient, hoping for rewards from Allaah advancing against the enemy and not fleeing from the 'battlefield." [1]

It happened when the enemy was standing in front of Muslims equipped with a mountain of military hardware, three times more personnel, and war animals. On top of it was the tribal pride. The enemy could not imagine a crashing defeat. Look at the response of leaders of Makkah when they received the "bad news of retreat". Mobarikpuri writes Salman bin Abdullah Khazai took the news of the battle. He went to Haram and announced, all the key figures of the Quraysh were killed. Hearing it Safwan Ibn-e-Ummiya was sitting in the Hateem said, I swear if he is in his senses, ask him about me. Where am I now? Salman indicated him, he is there

---

[1] Kandhelvi, Yusaf, Hayatus Sahabah, V. 1, p. 409.

in the Hateem. He said further, I have seen his father and a brother when they lost their lives.

The prophet (ﷺ) was encouraging soldiers because the result of the event could lay down the foundations of Islam till the day of Judgement. The prophet (ﷺ) supplicated before the encounter, O Allah, if this team would be martyred, no one would be there to worship you. [1] The challenge was to win the war. It was a critical occasion. The problem was limited resources. However, a win could open the door of opportunities. And as the history unfolded events, the prophet (ﷺ) enjoyed the victory. It leads towards the series of successes the prophet (ﷺ) had harvested in his lifetime.

The prophet's (ﷺ) action to resort to Allah (SWT) was an excellent choice. In fact, there was no one to help him. Therefore, there was no choice available. Consequently, Allah, the exalted announced, [Remember] when your Lord inspired to the angels, "I am with you, so strengthen those who have believed. I will cast terror into the hearts of those who disbelieved, so strike [them] upon the necks and strike from them every fingertip." [Al-Anfal: 12] and [Remember] when you asked help of your Lord, and He answered you, "Indeed, I will reinforce you with a thousand from the angels, following one another." [Al-Anfal: 9]

---

[1] Mubarikpuri, p. 296.

The inspiration to his companions and seeking help from Allah (SWT) shows his motivational strategy. A leader does it whenever he feels his colleagues need it.

Kreitner (2009) reported a best practice in motivation. Pat McGovern paid gratitude to his employees for the contribution they make for the organisation. He complimented someone for the column he wrote for a magazine. He calls upon people for the annual festival, requested feedback and congratulate for a specific achievement. Pays personal gratitude to every employee which were 1500 at the time of the report.

Leadership

The writers of the biography of the prophet (ﷺ) examined many dimensions of his leadership capabilities. Purpose seemed to me was to identify his capabilities as a successful leader. My objective is the same, but the perspective is a little bit different, to find out his abilities from the viewpoint of a leader of an organisation. It implies it includes all his merits because he had created a revolution. Managed it and prepared successors who look after his legacy very well. Someone asked a CEO, what is the primary task of a CEO? He said training / preparing his successor.

Allah (SWT) has appointed Muslims as a leader (manager) of this world[1]. When Muslims sacrifice for the pleasure of Allah (SWT), He bestows upon them the rewards in this world: material resources, victory, help, good name, money, property, government, or manager ship of land (Hameed Ullah, p. 109).

Hameed Ullah (p.315) states that the prophet (ﷺ) had declared one qibla, one law and a single leadership for all Muslims. Places of worship were same; rules were same, and the rewards were the same for elites and working class. The formers were treated equally with the later in all occupations. It implies managers and employees should be treated equally in terms of rewards, consultation and in other organizational or human matters. It is possible when merit prevails in all aspects of employment. For instance, selection based on knowledge, physical strength, honesty and twakkle on Allah (SWT); reward should be linked with performance; it may be financial or no-financial. Prophet (ﷺ) had handed over the key to Kaaba to the original keeper

---

[1] Allah has promised those who have believed among you and done righteous deeds that He will surely grant them succession [to authority] upon the earth just as He granted it to those before them and that He will surely establish for them [therein] their religion which He has preferred for them and that He will surely substitute for them, after their fear, security, [for] they worship Me, not associating anything with Me. But whoever disbelieves after that – then those are the defiantly disobedient. (An-Nur: 55)

to make him happy and in anticipation that he would manage it well based on his past performance/experience.

Given that let us see the opinion of contemporary scholars. According to them, leadership is a process of influencing others to pursue objectives. (Kreitner, 2009). Objectives may be personal or organisational. As I said elsewhere that Allah (SWT) had appointed the prophet (ﷺ) which means the help and support of Allah (SWT) was with him. It does not exist under normal conditions or with a non-Muslim manager. A Muslim manager can solicit it through creating the traits/qualities the prophet (ﷺ) had taught to us. We have seen in the pages of history the help of Allah (SWT) with the rightly guided caliphs and others. Umer (RA) while delivering the Jumma sermon shouted at Saariya (RA) about the position of the enemy army.

Influencing power

Islam applies the carrot and sticks approach to influence others including employees.[1] In addition, the prophet (ﷺ) had applied personal influence which he gained in his life. For instance, he was famous for truthfulness and honesty which made him a charismatic personality. He had exercised

---

[1] Management literature identifies five bases of power: rewards (financial or non-financial), coercive (power to punish), legitimate (formal power), referent (personal magnetism or charisma), and expert (the ability to dispense valued information).

them when he functioned as a business manager and at the occasion of the erection of Black Stone to Kaaba prior to the announcement of his prophethood.

He created trust and a symbol of a hardworking person during his business ventures to Syria. Mubarikpuri writes about his trade trip to Syria.

Muhammad (Peace be upon him), had no job (Permanent type of job) at his early youth, but it was reported that he worked as a shepherd for Bani Sa 'd and in Makkah. At the age of 25, he went to Syria as a merchant for Khadijah (May Allah be pleased with her) Ibn Ishaq reported that Khadijah, daughter of Khwailid was a businesswoman of great honour and fortune. She used to employ men to do her business for a certain percentage of the profits. Quraish people were mostly tradespeople, so when Khadijah was informed of Muhammad (Peace be upon him), his truthful words, great honesty, and kind manners, she sent for him. She offered him money to go to Syria and do her business, and she would give him a higher rate than the others. She would also send her hireling, Maisarah, with him. He agreed and went with her servant to Syria for trade.

When he returned to Makkah, Khadijah noticed, in her money, more profits and blessings than she used to. Her hireling also told her of Muhammad's good manners, honesty, deep thought, sincerity, and faith.[1]

It suggests that the business venture brought forward the personal characteristics of the prophet (ﷺ). He had utilised them to gain higher outcome then other people who were engaged in business with Khadijah, the business-lady. It highlighted the differentiating features of the prophet (ﷺ), we can learn that mere feature does not play any role in a project unless they are utilised prudently.

Relationship management or Management by relations

Relationship marketing and relationship management are contemporary managerial concepts which evolved from the experience of scientific management to the behavioural school of thought. The journey started from the stick of bureaucracy to the carrot of human relations. It is because the human knowledge is limited; the limitation forced us to evolve with the passage of time, change of circumstances, needs, wants, level of education and other internal as well as external factors. Since the knowledge of the Creator is complete, therefore, the prescription was also complete which did not evolve over time. It prescribes the best of all in the first instance.

---

[1] P. 90

Prophet (ﷺ) had applied the managerial concepts which will be applicable till the end of the world. He left the "complete" management of humanity forever. If someone would have interpreted it today in the context of "relationship", it fulfils his demands. And the same will be true for the past as well as for the future.

The concept of relationship is being applied in management these days, thus, it is related to the managerial strategy of the prophet (ﷺ). It is worthwhile to remember the theory of relationships was introduced in the seventh century A.D., but its importance has been realized in the 21st century. The Prophet (ﷺ) had expanded his relationships by enhancing his family. He married from famous tribes within Makkah and from the Arab peninsula. The objective was to make allies and expand the influence of his organization/state. Hameed Ullah states the rationale of prophet's (ﷺ) marriages. Umat-ul-momaneen Javaria (RA) was the daughter of the head of the bani-almustaliq tribe. It was a huge and powerful tribe used to live between Makkah and Madinah. The marriage caused to increase the boundary of the organization about 100 miles (160 KM) towards the north and towards Makkah.[1] Two of the Umat-ul-momaneen belonged to Yamani tribe which was strong and respectable. The prophet (ﷺ) also established a familial relationship with a tribe called Kinda which was a

---

[1] Hameed Ullah, p. 136.

royal family established its government between northern Syria and northern Iraq. Two of them belonged to previously Jews and Christian families; these two marriages had shown that the holder of the book (Jews and Christen) shares some common threads with Islam i.e. the God is one and He had sent down their prophets (AS) and the previous books. The purpose was to demonstrate that Islam and the prophet (ﷺ) respects previous religions and marring their women is permissible. Establishing family relations with them put them on equal footings, respect, and honour. It eliminates the concept of superiority; the action practically announced the equality. Hameed Ullah provides references from Quran and Hadith to support the establishment of relations with Jews and Christians.

Role Model

The organization research suggests managers to be a role model to develop a relationship with employees to motivate them and to manage them. The prophet (ﷺ) was declared a role model in Quran to the nearest effect; he is the perfect role model for you to follow.[1] The prophet (ﷺ) himself

---

[1] There is indeed a good model for you in the Messenger of Allah - for the one who has hope in Allah and the Last Day and remembers Allah profusely. [Al-Ahzab: 21]

says to the nearest effect, you are supposed to follow me, my way of life and my guided Khulafa. [1]

Three examples may suffice the point. He used to do his personal jobs himself. Second, when the trench was mined at the occasion of the third battle with Quresh, he dug the trench himself. Third, he exempted him and his family from Zakat as beneficiaries of the Islamic tax. The prophet (ﷺ) had written off the interest of his uncle to eliminate the practice after the conquer of Makkah.

Accountability

Accountability is followed by responsibility and it creates accountability. All the prophets (AS) are given authority to propagate faith which turns into responsibility. Consequently, the prophets are accountable as described in Quran, we would ask the people (or nations) to whom the prophets were deputed in order to convey the message of Allah (SWT) and prophets (AS) would also be asked whether they had delivered the message as it ought to be (Al-A'raf:6). Muhammad (ﷺ) asked his companions at the last sermon about it. Weather he

---

[1] Narrated Abu Huraira: Allah's Messenger (ﷺ) said, "All my followers will enter Paradise except those who refuse." They said, "O Allah's Messenger (ﷺ)! Who will refuse?" He said, "Whoever obeys me will enter Paradise, and whoever disobeys me is the one who refuses (to enter it)." [Sahih al- Vol. 9, Book 92, Hadith 384]

delivered the message of Allah (SWT), all of them replied, yes "you have fulfilled its right / responsibility."

Establishment of Justice

The Prophet (ﷺ) has been ordained to establish justice (Ash Shura:15). Justice is a broad concept; it encompasses every sphere of life. In managerial terms, it includes assignment of jobs/functions, payment of remuneration, promotion based upon merit, and treating everyone equally to the best of his understanding. It encompasses all the aspects of modern human resource management. In other words, when justice prevails in an organization everyone would be motivated, satisfied, and enjoy his job. He is free to work and free to quit when he finds a better employment opportunity elsewhere.

Muslims in general and managers commonly ordained, to be honest; the honesty is required at three levels: with Allah, with His Prophet (ﷺ) and between Muslims (Al-Anfal: 27). Sympathy is a human feeling; it is something beyond rules and regulation. Quran ordains to deal with people sympathetically (An-Nisa': 58)

Consultation and involvement

Management literature emphasizes the involvement of employees, customer, partners, and suppliers. Participatory style of management got popularity during behavioural movement in the 1920s and later due to its support for the involvement of employees. Islam emphasizes the importance of involvement through consultation; a Muslim manager decides on the recommendations or suggestions of his team. It is associated with tawakkal, the dependence on Allah after deciding (Aal'-Imran: 159).

The hiring suggestion is for the pleasure of Allah (SWT) and in fact for Him. When a decision is made and announced; it implies the participants have accepted it and promised to implement it. The promise is with Allah (SWT) in the first instance; therefore, Allah (SWT) says to the nearest effect that you should fulfil the promise.[1]

---

[1] O you who have believed, fulfil [all] contracts. Lawful for you are the animals of grazing livestock except for that which is recited to you [in this Qur'an] - hunting not being permitted while you are in the state of ihram. Indeed, Allah ordains what He intends. [Al Ma'idah: 1]

2 SOCIAL RESPONSIBILITY

Introduction

Business organizations are part of society which demands them to participate in public affairs or welfare activities that enhance and contribute to national development and prosperity. It includes the production and distribution of user friendly and beneficial products. It also comprises charging reasonable prices, earning an acceptable amount of profit, and looking after customers.

In this connection, a part of the profit must be devoted to social activities such as cultural programs, charitable works and helping needy and poor people. Islam guides managers at the state level where to spend taxes. Appropriate salaries should be paid in the business organization so that the employees fulfil their needs out of them. Hazrat Umer (RA) paid a sizeable number of salaries to military and other personnel.

Albeit employees are not poor yet if some of them cannot meet their livelihood out of the remuneration they receive from their work should be entitled to receive extra money from the employer. The organization should set up a special fund for such employees. It would make them free from financial worries; such employees would concentrate on their jobs and become productive workers. Low paid employees often work for a second employer or work as self-employed. It impedes them to focus on their principal job; consequently, they rarely involve innovative activities or become productive personnel.

Purpose of social responsibility is to offer welfare activities, to save the public from harmful activities and artefacts. Creation of ability to think positively is also a part of it (Mashhadhi, 2005).[1] There are two aspects of it: individual and collective. The prophet (ﷺ) has taken some social measures as an individual and some as a head of the state. We discuss them in the following paragraphs.

Individual measures

There was a famous peace treaty signed before the announcement of prophethood called "Half-Alfazool". The prophet (ﷺ) participated in it and played an active role. It was the first major effort to

---

[1] Mashhadhi, Seyd Naveedul Hasan (2005) Rehmat-e-Alam aur Rafa-e-Aama [The Prophet (ﷺ) and his Welfare Activities], *Halal*, 41(30-33), 86-88.

protect and support the oppressed. It was important in the environment where might was always right. Tribal traditions were supporting the oppressors for the sake of tribe. The victim was suffering because he was weak, and the oppressors were oppressing because they were strong.

The prophet (ﷺ) never said no to anyone who asked for help. An old woman was carrying some baggage on the top of her head; the prophet (ﷺ) took her baggage and walked with her.

The worst enemy of Islam and notorious hypocrite Abdullah bin Ubai asked for the personal gears of the prophet (ﷺ) at his death bed. He assumed his agony would subsidise through wearing it. The prophet (ﷺ) had gifted him it.

The prophet (ﷺ) forgave all his opponents at the occasion of conquered of Makkah. He announced writing off all the interest (a large amount of money) due to his uncle Abbas (RA) from the debtors at the same occasion. He said to the nearest effect that the prophets (AS) do not leave behind any material thing; whatever they left it became charitable.

The prophet (ﷺ) also participated as a leader for the installation of the Black Stone at its designated position. The leaders of Makkah unanimously elected him the spearhead of the project. The prophet (ﷺ) resolved the matter amicably and democratically. It demonstrated the managerial ability of the prophet (ﷺ) while he was a young person.

Collective measures

The prophet (ﷺ) as the head of an organisation put forward a range of measures for the welfare of common people. There was a general scarcity of water in Madinah; the prophet (ﷺ) asked Usman (RA) for buying a well-known well of water and devoted it to public usage.

Marriage is one of the noblest ways to satisfy human desire absence of which opens the back door to fulfil it illegally. The prophet (ﷺ) encouraged it. He addressed to the young folk of the society and advised them to get married. However, some people could not make it due to financial constraints. The prophet (ﷺ) encouraged them and planned for their marriage. Rabi bin Ka'b (RA) described his story in detail. He said that the prophet (ﷺ) enquired of me about it (My marriage) many times. But I could not do due to financial problems. Then the prophet (ﷺ) arranged financial resources for his marriage.

Another important measure was the integration of migrants and Helpers in Madinah after migration. Principally they belong to diverse cultures; the Makkans were traders, and the people of Madinah were farmers. Secondly, the former left everything behind while the later were native and rich. The prophet (ﷺ) established brotherhood among them. The People of Madinah open hearty accepted them and generously shared their resources. It was such a great incident of the time that history could not fetch such an example right from its birth. The partnership of the two communities became exemplary.

In this connection, the prophet (ﷺ) had taken a new measure to pay tribute to the war effected people and leaders of opposing forces. He generously gifted them at the occasion of conquered of Makkah. The tradition was to snatch all the possession of the enemy and made slave unhurt human capital including children, women, and others. The prophet (ﷺ) did not destroy any property or natural resources. One writer appropriately said that he had incorporated humanitarian values in the battlefield first time in known history.

Saani (2016) summarised some other aspects of his social welfare actions.[1]

SOCIAL RESPONSIBILITY

Honouring the guest

---

[1] Saani, Javed Iqbal (2016) Responsibilities of Managers: Selected Ahadith, available on amazon.co.uk. (Paperback edition)

1. The prophet (ﷺ) said, "Anyone who believes in Allah and the Last Day should honour his guest."

2. The prophet (ﷺ) said, "Hospitality is for three days, and what is beyond that is sadaqa for him."

Setting free the captives

The Prophet (ﷺ) said, "Set free the captives e.g. Hawazin captives were set free.

3 PROPHET (ﷺ) AS AN INNOVATOR

Introduction

Drucker (1998) believes the basic function of a manager is marketing and innovation because "it is the means by which the manager (entrepreneur) either creates new wealth-producing resources or endows existing resources with enhanced potential for creating wealth."[1] In other words, innovation is "a new way of doing something." (Wikipedia). "Innovation involves the development and implementation of new ideas and practices (Dyck and Neubert, 2009)." New means producing, introducing, or discovering something the first time.

---

[1] Drucker, P F (1998) The discipline of innovation Harvard Business Review. 1998 76(6):149-57.

Practice refers to "a method, procedure, process, or rule used in a particular field or profession; a set of these regarded as standard."

The prophet (ﷺ) of Islam had introduced a range of economic, political, and social practices during his time. At the occasion of placement of the Black Stone, he involved the tribal leaders, consequently, all were happy, and the matter was resolved amicably. Although Islam was not a new faith because Allah, the exalted had revealed it to Adham (AS) thousands of years ago. The ingredients of the new faith were the same as they were assigned to the first man on the earth. However, Islam was considered the new edition of the previous version of the religion.

Islam was introduced as a social product in Makkah where there was a lot of resistance for its diffusion. It was an innovative idea (product) in that there were many Gods who were offering many solutions to their followers. Some were reserved for rain, some were for giving sons, some were providing sustenance etc. The idea of one God was new to everyone in Makkah. People could not believe that one God could possess all the qualities and capabilities acquired. The prophet (ﷺ) had implanted the idea.

Let us look at the erection of Black Stone. Since it was not possible to make changes in the product, the prophet (ﷺ) changed or introduced a new process. He put the object in his cloak and invited chiefs to hold a corner of it and carry it near the place of erection. All the participants were happy to put his share in the noble job. Prophet (ﷺ) had also applied/used the old tool, the cloak in a new way. It made it an innovation. The job was done differently, thus the strategy was also new. And as has been seen elsewhere it was a participative and democratic approach of management.

Later, he worked innovatively as a businessman which yielded handsome results. It was acknowledged by one of the businesspersons and offered him a business partnership. It ended the prophet's (ﷺ) marriage with her; she became the first lady (and a person) who embraced him as a follower of the prophet (ﷺ). It seemed an unprecedented achievement in his prophethood. And it functioned as a snowball for his mission, spreading the message of Allah (SWT) all over the world.

He used to spend days/weeks together in the cave for spiritual meditation. It was also an innovation because very few examples are found in the history of this kind. It not only strengthened his physical capabilities because he used to live in modest conditions, alone and without luxurious provisions. It also enhanced his spiritual power, a source of recognizing the true creator. His familiarity with spiritualism and practical training enabled him for the noble job he was assigned. It was a unique idea especially in the environment of multi-gods concept.

He was worshipping only one. It was making him different from others.

The prophet (ﷺ) had presented the new religion in a novel way in the environment of polytheism. His argument was for the support of oneness of Allah (SWT), the exalted. The people of Makkah were objecting the idea because they had fabricated hundreds of gods. Each of which was responsible for a certain function. The prophet (ﷺ) argued about the malfunction of the universe in case of polytheism. He said Creator is only one, other objects were created. The holy Quran put forward hundreds of examples to justify it. Since it was the universal fact, so the people accepted it after some resistance.

The prophet (ﷺ) did many jobs or completed various projects in an innovative manner. Some of the actions he did were of the supernatural category. They were known as miracles. They were also innovation; scholars believe the number of such miracles was about 300. However, I want to describe some others; they are related to his capacity as a management expert.

When he did hijrah, he adopted a unique way to travel to Madinah which was not a traditional route to the destination. At the occasion of the war of Trench, he dug a trench to build a line of defence. Such a war strategy was not in practice in the Arab land. It became one of the reasons for his success in the event. It was a success because the enemy could not dare to harm Muslims. Partly due to their inability to cross the trench. Had the enemy jumped in the trench, it would be easy prey for Muslims. He has also adopted a unique approach to propagate his idea through sending a group of his companions to Abyssinia. No one has used the strategy. It provided safety to the participants and introduced Islam to the new land. The Quraysh sent a team to complain about them to the king of the country. It enabled Muslims to explain their religion to the king and his cabinet. Consequently, he rejected the demand of Quraysh and offered extra favour to the refugees.

The prophet (ﷺ) had introduced a new way of life, an economic system, a political theory, and a social system for the entire humanity. His teachings revolutionised the world for ever. Impacts of his changes were felt in the four corners of the world then and till the Last Day.

The economic innovation

The economic system was based on interest; the wealth was concentrated in few hands. The "have" was openly exploiting the "have not". The interest was being charged at high rates; failure could lead to fortifications of personal belongings including the personal residence where one was living etc. The prophet (ﷺ) introduced the concept of interest free economy. Loans without interest and partnership in production and distribution of goods and services were the new rules. Sympathy was the corner stone of the new economic system.

The political system was based upon social justice and service to the community. And the improvised democratic system was installed where competent members of the society can vote to elect their representatives. Those who aspire for power were not appointed for the positions.

Entering the foreign markets

The people were opposing the "new product" openly and with full force. However, the idea was getting popular gradually despite opposition.

The Prophet (ﷺ) thought it should be exported where it might get acceptance i.e. Abyssinia where the prospective customers were not idolaters. The new customers were the people of the book who believe in Allah (SWT); they knew His prophets (AS). When Muslims migrated to Abyssinia, they were comfortable to introduce Islam and they were also free to practice their faith.

The migration offered an opportunity to travel to another country for the sake of Islam. They learnt how to deal with new circumstance and how to cope with difficult conditions. They demonstrated themselves as a separate social force and an ideological nation. Since they encountered similar difficulties, yet they inculcated solidarity and unity amongst themselves. They enjoyed an opportunity to present their ideology outside the Arab world and started to invite people of the book instead of idolaters. In this way, the message crossed the boundaries of Makkah and entered in the international phase **(Gilani,)**.[1]

The Prophet (ﷺ) had travelled to Taif, a nearby city and the home of some strong tribes to deliver his message. Although the expedition did not produce positive results instantly, later, they entered in the fold of Islam (the product). Muhammad bin Qasim, the general who conquered southern part of India, contemporary Pakistan, belonged to the city. From managerial and marketing perspective the product was exported from the hometown to the neighbouring areas, the unsatisfied part of the market. The uniqueness of the expansion was that all was accomplished without investing additional resources.

He travelled alone with a single human as a helper. What a courage it was, what a plan it was? He focused on "Opinion leaders", the foundation of modern marketing philosophy. As a salesperson, he was selling his ideas, the product he received from his Creator. The product was free from physical defects and there were no side effects. The product was providing complete health; there was a lifetime guarantee for the users.

---

[1] Gilani, Syed Manazir Hussan (1981) An-Nabi al khaatam, Maktaba Akhuwwat.

The seller was using the product himself; he did not promise benefits which he had not experienced. The presenter was trustworthy; the truth was on his right hand and honesty on the other hand. He had been tasted for forty years in the venue of the market, in the markets of Syria and Makkah. And among the critics who did not turn any stone to stop him from his marketing efforts. They had tried their strategy of greed, power, and other non-financial benefits. But he was free from personal benefits, in fact, he was promised to receive a reward from the heavens not on the face of the earth but in the gardens of paradise. When someone is free from the greed of commission then his devotion is personal, his vision is perfect, his efforts are endless, and his motivation is limitless. He knows not only the benefits of his product in the world but also in the Hereafter, the most important segment of life. He marketed his product with dual benefits and the cost was nothing but to believe in One Allah (SWT), the creator, the sustainer, and the guide.

He tried to sell the product to a wholesaler, but he did not receive a positive response from them, then he tried to sell it to the public directly. Although he did not capture market share immediately but captured the whole market later.

4 MANAGERIAL STRATEGIES

Introduction

The prophet (ﷺ) had adopted three steps while establishing the new state (the mega organization) and its financial system. They are.

1- Exemption of prophet (ﷺ) and his family from receiving financial benefits from the collection of Zakat (the annual tax).

2- The prophet (ﷺ) had established the mega organization from scratch. He did not inherit any system of government in Madinah or any establishment upon which he could build upon (Hameed Ullah, p. 138)

3- The prophet's (ﷺ) tremendous administrative achievement was the rehabilitation of migrants from Makkah and Abyssinia. Hameed Ullah says, "the management of the (rehabilitation) was simple, effective and pragmatic". (p.138)

Pro-active management style

A proactive manager continuously analyses the internal and external environment to find out any threat that may emerge on the horizon of the organization. He responds in time i.e. before the threats become dangers so that their possible negative consequences may be addressed. A prudent and vigilant manager makes it a routine as a part of his strategic intent.

The prophet (ﷺ) has taken a series of actions to safeguard the organization. It may be worthwhile to mention here the opinion of contemporary management theorists. They believe modern managers "must be proactive, anticipate change, and continually refine, and when necessary, make significant changes to their strategies" (Dess, Lumpkin and Eisner, 2006).[1] Muhammad (ﷺ) was a proactive manager, always anticipate change and take active accordingly. **Gilani (1981)** summarized his strategy as if any threat is emerging inside or outside the organization; ignoring it or did not anticipate it, did not consider it significant, then a small danger may become a significant threat which can jeopardize the existence of the organization. Thereafter, the leader, like a janitor, identifies threats, understand them, and take necessary measures to control them. Internal issues were addressed in time, the external issues were accepted

---

[1] (Dess, Gregory G, Gerry McNamara, and Alan Eisner (2006) Strategic Management: Creating Competitive Advantages, McGraw-Hill Education.

as challenges and removing them or minimizing their impacts. These are part of the responsibilities of a manager. Let us examine some of them.

At the occasion of war of trench, the third major encounter between non-believers and the Muslims, the Jew tribe called Bani Quraiza who was an ally of Muslims betrayed them; the prophet (ﷺ) put them under siege soon after the war and expelled them from Madinah. In addition, when Bani Quraiza dishonoured the truce, there was a possibility of their attack on Madinah while the Muslims were involved in the battle in the outer part of the city. The prophet (ﷺ) enquired through a high-level team of two chiefs of 'helpers' of Madinah about the intentions of the tribe. The prophet (ﷺ) had appointed a new Muslim, Naeem bin Masood as special ambassador to talk to Bani Quraiza, Quresh, and other Jews to weaken their alliance. The efforts were successful, and these parties fell apart; consequently, no one dares to launch a united invasion on the Muslim.

The truce of Hodhaibia also opened the doors for long term success. Although, the pact was a win for Makkans it became a source of expanding Islamic message. It quickly increased the number of Muslims and ended at the conquer of Makkah, the event that caused other tribes of the Arabian Peninsula to embrace Islam.

At the time of Badr, the prophet (ﷺ) has chosen to encounter enemy instead of following the trade caravan, an easy prey. The selection of right but aggressive target led to the defeat of Makkans. Consequently, the Muslims have recognized a military power, a threat, and a competitor. The war was the first step towards the dominance of Islam, a corner stone for the establishment of the mega organization i.e. the Muslim state of Madinah.

When the united forces of Makkans and other tribes invaded Madinah in the war of trench, the prophet (ﷺ) had analysed the scale of the strength of competitors. He felt the inability of his army to complete with the counterpart, a new strategy was put forward to encounter, the trench was dug as a defence line. The competitors had never encountered such a tactic, therefore, unable to articulate any competing strategy. Therefore, the prophet (ﷺ) won the war.

Innovative solution of problems

In business terms, it implies competing with an innovative solution when the competition is intense, and their resources are superior. According to Kotler & Armstrong (2014), [1] companies in terms of competition fall into four categories – leaders, challengers, followers, and niche servers. The mega organization was a challenger at that time; it was embracing the challenge posed upon them by the

---

[1] Kotler, Philip T., and Gary Armstrong (2014) Principles of Marketing, Pearson.

leader of the land because no one was challenging Makkans. Their resources were superior quantitatively. The prophet (ﷺ) and his mega organization were striving to become a leader. And the event was the turning point; the enemy returned without an open war at the war of trench. It encouraged Muslims to think about a counterattack or at least designing a strategy for it. The purpose was to sell their product to Makkans in the first instance and then to the Arab world and beyond. Another danger emerged when the hypocrites built a place of worship which could enable them to manufacture conspiracies peacefully in a cool place. Since the prophet (ﷺ) was divinely guided, he was informed about the reality of the new place; he demolished the centre of conspiracies.

Apart from disbelievers, the hypocrites were opposing the cause of Allah (SWT) significantly. However, the prophet (ﷺ) was not taking stern action against them, obviously, it was with the consent of Allah (SWT). At the occasion of the Tabuk expedition, the hypocrites were getting together at the home of a Jew and preventing people to participate in the battle. The prophet (ﷺ) allowed Muslim to burn out his home to abolish a centre of the conspiracy. Consequently, the hypocrites did not dare to establish another such centre.

The prophet (ﷺ) once visited a Jew tribe called Banu Nazir who planned to kill him through throwing a huge rock upon him. He came to know the conspiracy; therefore, forced them to leave the city. It diminished the internal threat for good. In addition, he established business (or political) relationships with neighbouring tribes to neutralize them against the external threat and or to make them ally for the same purpose. In strategic terms, it implies the development of joint ventures to compete against foreign products (in this case external parties i.e. Quresh). The prophet (ﷺ) had implemented the strategy in two phases: to neutralize them and made them an official ally. It was achieved as a dominant party which the terms of truce dictate us. For instance, the following terms were common conditions:

1- They were offered security and protection from external threat.

2- In case of war between the ally (the tribe under consideration) and its enemy the Muslims shall help them. It was applicable in case of any other type of aggression.

3- It was also applicable to the associated nomads travelling anywhere in the desert area. It extended the boundaries of the Muslim state because these people used to travel for and wide areas of Madinah. It implies wherever they would have some fight with any tribe the Muslim army could be involved. Since the Muslim army was an organized force, therefore, the change of its dominance was high.

4- Muslims believe that the ultimate helper is Allah (SWT). It suggests the ally tribes implicitly embrace the beliefs of Muslims.

These terms were attractive from the perspective of the partner tribes as well because they consider it an association with a powerful state. The Muslim umbrella used to provide the shadow they needed to live peacefully without fear or external danger. The prophet (ﷺ) was consolidating the scattered tribal power and was minimizing the opposition to bring them under the circle of harmony and cooperation. It brought peace and tranquillity through reduction of political disturbance, wars lordship, and tribal system. The country became a unified state later; it was professionally managed and was working under a single administration. It made it feasible to establish a civilized nation. Since major tribes or their branches joined the Muslim hands yet the Quraysh of Makkah were gradually isolated in the Arabian Peninsula. The consolidation strategy provided power, confidence, and dominance over time. It enabled the propagation of Islam through increased efforts of Dawah and Tabligh (invitation towards Islam, teaching, and learning activities).

It is followed by written correspondence campaign to kings or their representatives; many of them embraced Islam which strengthened the Islamic cause. Remaining tribes rushed to Madinah to listen to the prophet (ﷺ) and accept him as a prophet (ﷺ) of Allah (SWT). They took refuge under the flag of Islam because there was no other shelter where anyone could live in peace, harmony and fearlessly.

The Quresh were being defeated gradually; inclusion of each tribe was strengthening Muslim power and was weakening their strength. Consequently, when the prophet (ﷺ) took the decisive step to overcome them, Quresh was helpless, no one dared to join them or protect them. Quresh failed to establish a military power under one flag. They brought a huge army in the war of trench, but they were not under a single administration. Each tribe was a constituent unit which was free to leave the battle at any time. It was observed when they withdrew from the front line.

The strategic stance continued. The Makkans posed a challenge following an unfinished campaign of Uhad to have combat at the place of Badr next year in the same month. The prophet (ﷺ) took his companion and travelled to the designated place but Abu-Sufyaan, the than the leader of Quresh did not dare to face Muslims. However, it restored the proud of Muslims which they had weakened the year before.

5 FINANCIAL MANAGEMENT

Introduction

The prophet (ﷺ) has introduced a unique financial system for individuals and organisations. One factor was common, however, that is neither individual no organisations make transactions applying interest. It might be worthwhile to note that the pre-Islamic society was based upon polytheism and interest. Business decisions were made around interest. Consequently, the wealth was concentrated in a few hands. The poor were getting more destitute day by day. The rate of interest was extremely high. Poor used to borrow for personal use, but they had to return it with a heavy amount of extra payment. As a result, they could not get rid of the loan for years.

The prophet (ﷺ) had prohibited the transaction of interest. He set up an example for it and announced the elimination of interest of his uncle. Hundreds of people got relief immediately. And the community became free from the trouble of interest. Similarly, business organisations were not allowed to transact in interest. Most of the business organisations were either sole proprietorship or partnership at that time. The prophet (ﷺ) himself worked in a business partnership with Khadijah (RA). Islam encouraged such forms of business to enhance social bindings in society. Cooperation and trust were the fundamentals of organisations.

Sources of finance

Many measures were put in practice at the government level. The foundation of it was the system of Zakat and ownership of property. The later was associated with the concept of halal and haram. One can own wealth through halal means. The business community was motivated to earn a reasonable amount of profit because a Muslim businessman makes money and earns a good deed at the same time.

The prophet (ﷺ) employed work force to collect zakat in the area the Muslim state was controlling. Jizya was collected from the non-Muslim community to provide them with security. The government had some share in war booty which was spent upon needy and poor subjects. In addition, the farmers need to share their crops with the government. The purpose was to collect from the "have" and distribute it to the "have not". It increased the circulation of wealth and created economic equality in society. The system took a few years only to reach to a level where it was hard to find any deserving person for spending money i.e. the recipient of Zakat.

The system of Zakat was simple and easy to manage. It is simple because if someone possesses a given amount of money or gold and silver, he/she needs to pay 2.5% of it. The government decides to collect it from those who can pay it. Since it is compulsory upon the rich, therefore, the government has not made efforts to convince people for payment. It is the responsibility of the person concerned; a religious duty of every Muslim to pay it. In short, the major sources of revenue of a Muslim government are zakat, usher (1/10th of the agricultural produce), one-fifth of spoils of war and protection tax from non-Muslim subjects.

Areas of spending

The government spends money on various welfare projects. Allah, the exalted says,

> The alms are only for the poor and the needy, and those who collect them, and those whose hearts are to be reconciled, and to free the captives and the debtors, and for the cause of God, and (for) the wayfarers; a duty imposed by God. God is Knower, Wise. [At-Tobah: 60]

It includes the wages of those who collect the revenue. In effect, they are the employees of the state. Another category is the new Muslims. The prophet (ﷺ) had distributed an ample number of spoils of war at the occasion of conquered of

Makkah. The purpose was to stabilise them on the new religion. Although it was not the immediate occurrence at that moment previously the companions were expelled from their home when they embraced Islam. It is also true these days. I have experienced such examples in the UK. In the case of a Muslim government, such gifts or financial support enables new Muslims to stick with the religion.

Another significant area for spending is to support those who are in debt. It could be personal as well institutional. So, the government must pay the debts of defaulters. One kind of defaulters is the captives who are unable to pay, for instance, ransom etc. The state can use the collected money to pay the amount demanded to get the captives free.

The alternative to the interest free banking is partnership and interest free loans. A well-known organisation in Pakistan advances a small amount of money to small traders. The recipient is supposed to return capital only. However, if he wants, he can pay a small amount as a contribution to the fund. One of the promoters or founding member said we started with the small amount of capital, but we have million in our possession. He further said that our recovery was more than 99%. In addition, interest free banks are successfully working all over the world. Many of them are also financing the housing sector in Britain and elsewhere.

Circulation of wealth

The purpose of circulation of wealth at the national level is to create equality, it should not be in the hands of few hands who exploit other for their own benefit. Modern economic theorists arrived at this reality after years of reach and experience. Islam had given the principle of distribution of wealth a long time ago. Quran says it should not circulate among wealthy people only.[1] When it changes hands it creates value, jobs, and wellness/prosperity. Fiscal and financial policies are articulated to achieve this objective. Purpose of the tax system is to collect money from rich people and spend on national projects such as building and construction of roads and bridges. Consequently, people find jobs and entrepreneurs find business opportunities. When individuals got employed, they spend on their needs and wants, and it increases prosperity.

The principle is also applicable at the organizational level. For instance, implementation of a fair wage system where everyone receives his due for his contribution in the generation of revenue and profit enables more circulation. In enhances with the

---

[1] That which Allah giveth as spoil unto His messenger from the people of the townships, it is for Allah and His messenger and for the near of kin and the orphans and the needy and the wayfarer, that it become not a commodity between the rich among you. And whatsoever the messenger giveth you, take it. And whatsoever he forbiddeth, abstain (from it). And keep your duty to Allah. Lo! Allah is stern in reprisal. (Al-Hashr: 7)

payment of bonuses and special allowance for increased performance. Sharing profit, equity, and contribution of the entrepreneur in the welfare of employees such as opening schools for their families, establishing hospitals, paying pension and gratuity etc.

Muslim manager ensures such a system in their organization so that wealth may be circulated among the workforces. An equitable remuneration structure fulfils the demands of justice as mentioned elsewhere. The employer should share profit because, it is the outcome of employees' relentless efforts.

Modern fiscal management or manager deals with the acquisition, application, and distribution of finance (funds). The acquisition is through revenue generation i.e. sales of products or rendering of services, borrowing from internal or external sources or reinvestment of earnings. Resources are applied for capital investments, working capital, and various expenses. Purpose of all is to generate revenue. Financial resources are distributed to shareholders, partners, creditors, or payment of long-term loans. Some are transferred to reserve or retained earnings to show the financial strength of the organization. These funds are also used for internal financing or reinvestment.

There was no organized financial system in Makkah because the focus was on individual development to cope with the collective system to be established in

Madinah. The prophet (ﷺ) had borrowed the she-camel from Abu-Bakr for the Hijrah expedition. It is the first financing activity for the cause of Islam. However, a well-organized financial system was established in Madinah. The system started with a volunteer contribution for wars. The booty was a capital gain emerged as an outcome of the war; it was distributed as per instructions of Allah (SWT). It was followed by the introduction of compulsory taxes like Zakat and Usher for mineral production. The beneficiaries were poor people in addition to collectors and new Muslims as outlined in Sura Toba. It seems beyond the scope of this book to investigate the Islamic financial system for which specialized works are available. Our purpose is to establish the fact that the prophet (ﷺ) was not only the pioneer of the financial system but also managed the financial affairs as an experienced financial manager. He institutionalized the honesty, trust, and selflessness for the service of society at large and the Muslim community specifically. This system matured during the government of Hazrat Umer (RA) when poverty was replaced with prosperity.

6 DECISION MAKING

Introduction

As we have seen in the development of his management thoughts there was a parliament of Quraysh prior to the prophet (ﷺ). It suggests the sense and importance of collective decisions. He had also made a democratic decision when he leads erecting the Black Stone. Democratic decisions enable people to participate in the resolution of issues associated with them. It suggests that the idea of democracy was already in his subconscious. Allah, the exalted is the creator of humans, He has created the desire of involvement of people for their day-to-day matters. Consequently, He commanded His prophet (ﷺ) to consult his companions to make decisions. And then count upon Him. Trust Him. He will make it fruitful if He wishes. His Will would come into existence, no matter what decision is made. Decision making is the act of identifying and choosing among alternative courses of action (Kreitner, 2009).

Given the above means, the prophet (ﷺ) had made scores of decisions in his life. It is notable to know that he was presenting the new religion to the people of Makkah in the first instance and rest of the world to humans and jins up to the Day of Judgement. In addition, Allah, the exalted was guiding him about the timing and structure of his decisions. For instance, he had presented his religion (product in terms of business) in various phases.

He did it secretly for the first three years as per the command of Allah (SWT). He announced to the world in the second phase. Looking at from the geographical point of view he started locally, expanded it to the national level and then reached the international level.
In other words, he commenced in Makkah, expanded to Taif and Madinah, and exported to Abyssinia.

Identifying and choosing alternatives

The prophet (ﷺ) had identified the targets for his religion. People of Makkah, the pilgrims of Madinah and a strong tribe of Taif. Also, the people of Abyssinia; the king was the focus. The later incidents showed that his imagination was correct. Although the people of Taif and Abyssinia did not take shelter under his umbrella, yet people of Madinah did it. As a result, it became the centre of his efforts and served as the first headquarter of Islam i.e. his idea.

He had selected many successful courses of action. First when he followed the trade caravan of Quraysh prior to Badr, the decisive armed encounter with Quraysh. He let the caravan and faced the enemy army. The outcome was in his favour. Second times, with the consultation of his companions, he left the city and welcome the enemy outside Madinah at the occasion of the expedition of the war of Trench. The result again favoured him. His third choice at the time of Hodhabia pact was to go for peace treaty rather than umrah; it also yielded victory.

Structured and unstructured decision

Structured decisions are of routine nature which is repeated frequently. Therefore, they are called programmed decisions. The decision maker follows a set of rules. The prophet (ﷺ) used to encounter various situations. The decisions to deal with criminal matters were straightforward. He had to determine the reality of the incident through evidence. For example, the confession of the concerned person/party. The punishment for adultery was to stone him/her as advised in the sharia law.

Nevertheless, he had to do unstructured decision with the consultation of his companions or the team of people involved. They were made in complex situations. At the occasion of Uhad, he accepted the proposal of companions. He did not follow them in Hodabia. The prophet (ﷺ) decided, and he firmly implemented it. Some of the companions were not agreed about the terms of the treaty. Allah, the exalted sent His command, it is not necessary or appropriate for the prophet (ﷺ) to accept the opinion of his colleagues.

Decision rules

Allah, the exalted provided a generic principle for the prophet (ﷺ) and his followers for good to make decisions. The example was given about the consumption of alcohol. Allah, the exalted said to the nearest effect that there are some benefits in it, but its harms are more than them. So, it is prohibited.[1]

The decisions may be made through consultation as ordained in Surah Shoorah.[2] The third principle for every member of the management team was to "obey" your appointed leaders until they do not make decisions against the sharia law. Thus, the leader can decide without consultation.

Prophet's way of making decisions

The prophet(ﷺ) used to call a meeting of his cabinet or shurah. Brainstorm the situation;

---

[1] They question thee about strong drink and games of chance. Say: In both is great sin, and (some) utility for men; but the sin of them is greater than their usefulness. And they ask thee what they ought to spend. Say: that which is superfluous. Thus, Allah maketh plain to you (His) revelations, that haply ye may reflect. [Al-Baqarah: 219]
[2] And those who answer the call of their Lord and establish worship, and whose affairs are a matter of counsel, and who spend of what We have bestowed on them. [Ash-Shurah: 38]

assorted options came forward and a decision was made. At the occasion of prisoners of war of Badr, he invited options of his colleagues. Umer (RA) put forward one of the famous options; they should be handed over to their close relatives and they should kill them. Abu Bakker (RA) suggested that they should be set free for an appropriate amount of ransom. Other options would have come. The prophet (ﷺ) opted the later view of Abu Bakker (RA).

The prophet's (ﷺ) decisions were flexible to accommodate the suggestion of his companions. At the occasion of Badr, the prophet (ﷺ) changed the position of the army upon the suggestion of a companion. [1]

It is important to understand that knowledge is required to make informed decisions. Kreitner (2009)[2] believes that knowledge management (KM) is necessary for informed decisions. KM is a strategy to acquire, preserve and disseminate information. It includes tacit and explicit knowledge. Tacit knowledge "is personal, intuitive, and undocumented information about how to skilfully perform tasks, solve problems, and make decisions.".

The holy Quran and his sunnah was the explicit knowledge. Both of which were documented. The

---

[1] Mubarikpuri, p, 288.
[2] P. 217.

holy Quran was preserved as soon as a part of it was revealed. It was compiled during the caliphate of Usman bin Affan (RA). The sunnah was documented later. The third source of explicit knowledge was the actions of his companions. And the final source is the agreement of religious scholars about a given matter.

Allah, the exalted had bestowed upon the prophet (ﷺ) special tacit knowledge. Once some people from outstripping of Madinah came to him and requested him to send some people for teaching and learning of Islam. The prophet (ﷺ) hesitated to do so and expressed his doubt and unwillingness about the request. But these people insisted; he sent a team of about 70 companions. The hosts betrayed and martyred them. The prophet's (ﷺ) doubt changed into the reality. [1]

Group decisions

Sometime more than one person is involved in a decision. Such decisions are common these days and are a current way to resolve issues. Judicial system follows it, political decisions are made in an equivalent way. Business decisions are also made in the same pattern.

Allah, the exalted had appointed the prophet (ﷺ) which means he was overall for decision making. But his nation was to teach the prophet's (ﷺ) lifestyle,

---

[1] Kandhelvi, Zakerya, p. 91-92.

therefore, Allah, the exalted instructed him to consult his companions. He has appointed a team to manage the affairs of Yemen. They were making (most probably) the group decisions i.e. through consulting each other.

Long term and short-term decisions

Businesses, government institutions, and even families need to decide according to the time. Management of a business organisation, as the experts have classified, make short-term, medium-term, and long-term decisions. The decision which encompasses one fiscal year is known as short term; medium term ranges from 1-3 years. And beyond that period, is considered long term.

The prophet (ﷺ) had made long term derision when he visited Taif. His perceived customers did not buy his idea. Instead, they showed severe hostility towards him and his message (product). The angles were on the command of the prophet (ﷺ), but he believed that if the people of Taif did not entertain me. Their coming generations would do. Therefore, it was a long-term decision.

The history had witnessed that it did not take long for the people of Taif to take refuge under the shade of Islam. One of Taifian general took the message of his prophet (ﷺ) to the Indian subcontinent. They are more than 600 million Muslims residing in the region today. Look at the implications of his long-term decision.

Another famous long-term decision was signing the treaty of Hodhabia. Its long-term benefits were realised soon. The message of Islam spread quickly around the Arab land. Take only the number of soldiers at Hodhabia and in conquer of Makkah; increased from 1400 to 10000 in two years. The decision in terms of time falls under the medium term. The treaty remained effective for two years or so.

The speciality of prophet's decisions

There are many characteristics of the decisions of the prophet(ﷺ). He was under the guidance of Almighty Allah, the exalted. It implies that he could not make an unrealistic decision especially when he made unstructured decisions. As we know such decisions need intuition and application of tacit knowledge. The history informed us that all his decisions were fruitful. At the military front, Muslims met a partial failure in Uhad. It was destined in the first instance but, it was due to the absence of the troops which he had appointed at an important pass. Most of his decisions were about political, military, and social matters (Integration of Helpers and Migrants) but his business decisions which he made prior to the announcement of his prophethood were also successful. His profitable business tours to Syria were proven evidence of his success.

7 CULTURAL CHANGES

Introduction

Culture is the way people behave with each other. It includes the language they speak, the dress they wear and the way they eat and drink. Put it in a formal way it is a pattern of basic assumptions which are discovered, invented, or developed. They are considered valid and taught to the new members as a correct way to perceive, think and feel. The purpose is to address problem especially external adoption and internal integration (Schein, 1985).[1] It includes the habits, prevailing attitudes, and grown-up pattern of accepted and expected behaviour

---

[1] Schein Edgar H (1985). Organizational culture and leadership, San Francisco: Jossey-Bass Publishers.

(Drennen, 1992).[1] This is the way things are and this is why they ought to be as they are (Bate, 1994). [2]

It suggests that it is the behavioural characteristics that are invented, discovered, or developed. Alternatively, what is the desirable behaviour or ought to be? Consequently, if some elements of the required behaviour are missing. The job of a manager is to create a behavioural pattern that should conform to the desired or required behaviour.

The emphasis is on the required behaviour. But it is common to experience that newcomers must adopt the cultural of the organisation where they start their work or membership. The holy prophet (صلى الله عليه وسلم) set up the organisation of Islam in Makkah. Allah, the exalted had defined the required behaviour. The prophet (صلى الله عليه وسلم) had adopted and institutionalised it to all levels of the organisation.

Let us see what the desired organisational culture was and way the prophet (صلى الله عليه وسلم) shaped it right from the inception of his mission. I am going to examine it in the following pages.

---

[1] Drennan, D., (1992). Transforming company culture, London: McGraw-Hill.
[2] Bate, S. (1994). Strategies for Cultural Change, Oxford: Butterworth Heinemann.

Change in belief.

The fundamental change was required in belief because the culture was shaped based on it. The prophet (ﷺ) coined the idea that Allah, the exalted is one. He is the creator of every living or non-living thing. He is the creator of conditions: happiness or sadness, richness or poorness, health, or sickness and so on. It was the basic trigger of all actions while behaviour is the collection of all those actions. The change was very bitter for the recipient, but they embraced it after some resistance.

Mutual respect

The second most important value was mutual respect. He announced during the last hajj. Your money and blood are as sacred as this day, month and the city are. It is applicable to every individual including shepherds and team/groups. He defined the authority of it at various levels. Since daughters were a cause of shame and humility, the prophet (ﷺ) said whosoever would raise a girl, he would be near to me on the Last Day. In the last sermon, he emphasised the rights of women. He said to the nearest effect that the paradise is under the feet of your mothers. Allah, the exalted said women are His breeding fields. In terms of employees, he said to the nearest effect *pay wages* before the perspiration sweat the worker.

> 'Abdullah ibne- 'Umar Radiyallahu 'anhuma narrates that Rasulullah (ﷺ) said: Pay the

labourer his wages before his sweat dries. (Ibne-Majah) [Muntakhib Ahadith, p.478]

It is their right and a way of respect from the employer point of view.

Promote greeting
378. Abu Hurairah (May Allah be pleased with him) reported: Messenger of Allah (PBUH) said, "By Him in Whose Hand my soul is! You will not enter Jannah until you believe, and you shall not believe until you love one another. May I inform you of something, if you do, you love each other. Promote greeting amongst you (by saying Assalamu `alaikum to one another)". [Riyadhus Saliheen, Abridged edition, Hadith 427, p.279]

Obeying manager/boss
2-Abu Musa Al Ash'ari (RA) narrates that Rasulullah (ﷺ) said: <u>Undoubtedly reverence to Allah includes honouring a grey-haired Muslim: and also the one who has memorised the Qur'an and he neither exceeds the proper bounds and nor does he turn away from it, and honouring a just ruler.</u> (Abu Dawud) [Muntakhib Ahadith, p.442]

3-Abu Bakra (RA) narrates: I heard Rasulullah (ﷺ) saying: <u>He who honours a king appointed by Allah</u>

<u>Tabaraka wa Taala in the world, Allah will honour him on the Day of Resurrection</u>. He who dishonours a king appointed by Allah (SWT) in the world, Allah will dishonour him on the Day of Resurrection. (Musnad Ahmad. Tabarani. Majma -'uz-Zawaid) [Muntakhib Ahadith, p.443]

Honesty

Honesty is another important value in the workplace. It is a bridge where management and employees stand on each side.

> Muzhim bin Zufar said, "Umar bin 'Abdul-'Aziz said to us, 'There are five qualities (which a judge should possess), and if he does not have one of them then he has one defect; and those qualities are: He must be an intelligent, patient, honest, stern and a learned religious scholar and knowledge seeking.'"[Al-Bukhari, Volume 9, p. 174]

Visiting sick

The prophet (ﷺ) suggested his followers/mangers walk the extra mile to win over the hearts. For instance, visit them when they fall *sick*, be courteous with them, offer good advice, give productive support whenever possible.

> Jabir (RA) narrates that Rasulullah (ﷺ) said: Anyone with these three qualities shall be

under the shade of Allah's Mercy (on the Day of Resurrection) and will be admitted into Paradise:

(I) Courtesy towards the weak

(2) Compassion to parents

(3) Kindness to slaves (subordinates). (Tirmidhi) [Muntakhib Ahadith, p. 402]

Abu Hurairah (May Allah be pleased with him) reported: I heard Messenger of Allah (ﷺ) saying, "Whosoever visits an ailing person or a brother of his to seek the Pleasure of Allah, an announcer (angel) calls out: `May you be happy, may your walking be blessed, and may you be awarded a dignified position in Jannah". [At-Tirmidhi, Riyadh Saleheen, Hadith Number 362]

Offering good advice

1-Narrated Jarir bin 'Abdullah: I gave the Pledge of allegiance to the Prophet (ﷺ) that I would listen and obey, and he told me to add: 'As much as I can and will give *good advice* to every Muslim.' [Al-Bukhari, Volume 9, Book 89, Hadith Number 311]

2-Adi bin Hatim (May Allah be pleased with him) reported: Messenger of Allah (peace be upon him) said, "Guard yourselves against the Fire (of Hell) even if it be only with half a date-fruit (given in charity); and if you cannot afford even that, you should at least say a good word." [Al-Bukhari & Muslim, Riyadh Saleheen, Hadith Number 693]

Giving good counsel

1-Abu Ruqayya Tamim ibn Aws ad-Dari reported the Prophet, may Allah (ﷺ) bless him and grant him peace, said, "The deen is good counsel." We said, "For whom?" He said, "For Allah, His Book, His Messenger, the Imams of the Muslims and their common people." [Al-Bukhari and Muslim, Riyad-us-Saliheen Hadith Number 181]

2-Jarir ibn 'Abdullah said, "I gave allegiance to the Prophet (ﷺ), may Allah bless him and grant him peace, on the basis of performing the prayer, paying the zakat and giving good counsel to every Muslim." [Al-Bukhari and Muslim, Riyad-us-Saliheen Hadith Number 182].

3-Anas reported that the Messenger of Allah, may Allah bless him and grant him peace, said, "None of you can truly be said to believe until he wants for his brother what he wants for himself." [Al-Bukhari and Muslim, Riyad-us-Saliheen Hadith Number 183]

Supporting subordinates

1-Ibn 'Umar reported that the Messenger of Allah, may Allah bless him and grant him peace, said, "The Muslim is the brother of the Muslim. He should not wrong him nor surrender him to his enemy. Allah will take care of the needs of anyone who takes care of the needs of his brother. On the Day of Rising Allah (SWT) will dispel the anxiety of anyone who dispels the anxiety of another Muslim. On the Day of Rising, Allah will veil anyone who veils another Muslim." [Al-Bukhari and Muslim, Riyad-us-Saliheen (Abridged edition) Hadith Number 135, p. 94]

2-Abu Hurayra reported that the Prophet (صلى الله عليه وسلم), may Allah bless him and grant him peace, said, "Allah will relieve anyone who relieves a believer of one of the afflictions of this world, of one of the afflictions of the Day of Rising. Allah will give ease in this world and the Next to anyone who eases the hardship of another. Allah will veil anyone who veils another Muslim in this world and the Next. Allah will help His slave as long as His slave is helping his brother." [Muslim, Riyad-us-Saliheen (Abridged edition) Hadith Number 145, p. 100]

3-Abu Hurayra reported that the Prophet (ﷺ), may Allah bless him and grant him peace, said, "'Someone who strives on behalf of widows and the poor is like someone who fights in the way of Allah.' I think that he also said, 'And like someone who continually stands at night in prayer and like someone who continually fasts.'" [Muslim and Bukhari, Riyad-us-Saliheen Hadith Number 265]

4-Abu'd-Darda' 'Umaymir said, "I heard the Messenger of Allah (ﷺ), may Allah bless him and grant him peace, say, 'Help me in seeking out the weak. They are supported. You are provided for on account of the weak among you." [Abu Dawud, Riyad-us-Saliheen (Abridged edition) Hadith Number 153, p. 104]

Merit based Selection and recruitment

Selection and recruitment must be based on merit (See exhibit)

HIRING

Appointment of a successor

The prophet (ﷺ) appointed his successor; he referred a woman to Abu Bakr in case of his absence.

Motivating for a certain leader/appointee

The prophet (ﷺ) persuade people for the appointment of a leader/manager

Peer approval/support

Umer motivated people to embrace the leadership/caliphate of Abu Bakr. He described his qualities: companion, association in the cave (past achievements/performance), evaluated (peer evaluation) that he was the most entitled person among us.

Appointment of a team

The prophet (ﷺ) has sent a team of governors to Yemen.

Appointment of advisors

1. Allah gives truthful subordinates /advisors who

help him towards good and vice versa

2. Allah sends prophets (and they their caliphs) and appoints advisors for them

Terms of employment

Allah's apostle took the oath for obedient to the manager in addition to other things like believing in the oneness of Allah, not stealing, not doing adultery, not killing children, and not accusing an innocent person.

Selection of caliph by experts

Usman bin Affan (RA), the third caliph, was selected caliph by a team of sahabah though a long consultation

Learning organisation
TRAINING

Basics

1. Teaching the knowledge of Quran and hadith is desirable for a Muslim and a manager

2. Teaching by doing is advisable as shown by the prophet (ﷺ) himself

3. The prophet (ﷺ) used to teach individually as well as collectively

4. Repeating essential elements thrice was the noble practice of the prophet (ﷺ); greeting thrice was also his practice

5. The prophet (ﷺ) was speaking very clearly so everyone could understand

6. A father's best gift for his children is good words (therefore, a manager's as well)

Short training sessions

7. Make prayers short so training session as well

8. It is derivable to have short lectures/sessions

Role model

MANAGER AS ROLE MODEL

1. The prophet's (ﷺ) character was the best example (model) for anyone who wants to follow him

2. The prophet (ﷺ) did not show disappointment, or sadness to his employee (e.g.

Ans (RA)) who served him for ten years

3. Piety (being religious) is a good character

4.'The best of you are the best in character.'

5. Good character is heavier on the Day of Rising and Allah dislikes foul language

6. The people of Garden are fearful to Allah and of good character

7. The best of you are best towards your wives (subordinates)

8. Good character is like fasting and prays at night

9. The prophet (ﷺ) gave a gift of a person who behaved him rudely

10. In response to people who struck and wounded him, he supplicates for their forgiveness

11- Patience is at the first stroke of a calamity

Managing issues
MANAGING ISSUES/DISPUTES

How to deal with mistakes?

1-The person urinated in the mosque was forgiven

and the prophet (ﷺ) said to make things easy for people and do not put them in difficulty.

2-One sahabi answered the sneezing of another person in salat but he said "he did not rebuke me, hit me, or abuse me. He merely said, 'It is not fitting to have any speech from people in the prayer. It is only glorification and proclaiming Allah great and reciting the Qur'an".

Accountability

1. Zakat collector was asked to deposit his gifts in the 'Baitul maal', the state treasury

2. On the Day of Rising, the managers will undergo a strict accountability

Not taking revenge

1. The prophet (ﷺ) did not take revenge for personal matters; he liked an easier way to deal with permitted actions

2. The prophet (ﷺ) did not take revenge from the people of Taif who stoned him

3. The prophet (ﷺ) did not strike anyone with his hand except in case of the rule of Allah is violated

4. The strong man is the one who controls his anger

5. Allah likes those who maintain good relations with those who do not treat them well

Equality

1. The prophet (ﷺ) has said about a legal verdict that if my daughter would have done the crime, I would decide against her

2. It is advised to give the same gifts to children (similarly employees)

3. The prophet (ﷺ) likes people who divide provision equally

Policy of punishment

The prophet (ﷺ) punished who remained behind in the war of Tabuk by social boycott.

Resolving disputes

1. Resolving issues between two people is equivalent to sadaqa

2. Promoting good (between people) including putting things right is recommended

3. It is disliked to not to do good

4. The prophet (ﷺ) settled many disputes between people

Ethics
MANAGING ETHICS

Fulfilling promise

One of the signs of a hypocrite is not fulfilling his promise.

Abu Bakr fulfilled the promise made by the prophet (ﷺ)

Consistency of actions

It is not recommended to start some good deed and then stop it after some times.

Helping subordinates

1. The prophet (ﷺ) says" On the Day of Rising Allah will dispel the anxiety of anyone who dispels the anxiety of another Muslim. On the Day of Rising, Allah will veil anyone who veils another Muslim."

2. The Prophet (ﷺ), may Allah bless him and grant him peace, said, "Allah will relieve anyone who relieves a believer of one of the afflictions of this world, of one of the afflictions of the Day of Rising. Allah will give ease in this world and the Next to anyone who eases the hardship of another".

3. The Prophet (ﷺ), may Allah bless him and

grant him peace, said, "'Someone who strives on behalf of widows and the poor is like someone who fights in the way of Allah.' I think that he also said, 'And like someone who continually stands at night in prayer and like someone who continually fasts.'"

4. Messenger of Allah(ﷺ), says, 'Help me in seeking out the weak. They are supported. You are provided for on account of the weak among you."

Organisation policy
ORGANISATIONAL POLICIES
Safeguarding rights of others

The best among you is the one "From whose: tongue and hands, other Muslims are safe".

Justice

The most excellent amongst the people is the one who is "Muttaqi (fearful of Allah) is pure of heart, free of sins and without injustice, hatred or jealousy for anyone".

Performance measurement

When neighbour say that a certain person is good (doing charitable deeds) he is so and vice versa

Paying remunerations

1. Rasulullah (ﷺ) said: Pay the labourer his wages before his sweat dries

2. The prophet (ﷺ) will be an opponent on the day of judgement "who employs a labourer and takes full work from him but does not pay him for his labour."

Other Values

The prophet (ﷺ) had introduced a system of values which makes the Islamic culture. Islam does not differentiate between organisational life and social life. Both are two dimensions of a coin. Also, Islam considers family as a small organisation or the first organisation a human encounter. The business organisation is the second level of the organisation while the country is the largest of these entities. Therefore, values developed and practiced at the smallest level are also applicable at other levels.

Islam also considers the individual as the basis of all activities because individuals become organisations and they make up the society. However, certain values are particular to the organisational activities. For instance, punctuality. It is necessary to create and maintain control. Islam also emphasises it. Some type of it is optional and others mandatory. Attending five times daily salah is compulsory but one can join the congregation in a time bracket. If fajr is prayed 6 am in the masjid, the individual can perform it between sub-e-sadiq and sun rise. In other words, there is a starting time and an ending time for each prayer. But congregation shall be at a fixed time. Similarly, fasting and performance of hajj are time bound. It implies that the individual is trained right from his childhood for punctuality. When the person joins his formal work, the punctuality does not seem to him a new "requirement".

One of the key factors in management is the spirit of acceptance/obedience. Islam emphasises it from the first day; it makes management of people easy. Islam also promotes team consciousness. It is compulsory to pray salah in congregation provided there is no strong excuse. Jummah prayer provides an opportunity for Muslims to get together on weekly basis.

A celebration of Eid is part of it. Allah, the exalted says to his prophet (ﷺ) to the nearest effect that does a consultation with your colleagues. These examples suggest that Islam encourages team spirit. The idea is to create a sense of collectively.

Quality management

The sense of quality is also a part of it. Contemporary experts realised the concept of quality in in the 20th century while the prophet (ﷺ) of Islam talked about it in the 7th century. Most of the quality parameters were put forward at that time. For instance, service quality emphasises on consistency. The prophet (ﷺ) said that "Abu Hurairah narrated that the Messenger of Allah (ﷺ) said: "Take on only as much as you can do of good deeds, for the best of deeds is that which is done consistently, even if it is little." [Sunan Ibn Majah, Vol. 5, Book 37, Hadith 4240]

Showing by doing

Take part in collective jobs once it was decided to cook food during a journey. The prophet (ﷺ) collected firewood. The companions said we would do. He said I did not like differentiation. Here are some more examples.

- He was an active participant in the battle of Uhad.
- Share ride of a camel with his companions in the journey
- He was a caring husband. An affectionate father and a helpful member of his family.
- The prophet (ﷺ) was an attractive personality; one reason was his humorous way of communication. But it does not cross

the boundary of ethnics or his status of prophethood.

The following exhibit summarises key values of an organisation that should be managed on the bases of Islamic principles.

Exhibit Summary of Islamic values	
Value	**Description**
Change in belief	Allah is one
Mutual respect	Money and blood of every Muslim is sacred to others
Greeting	Everyone should greet others
Obey managers/employers	It is a part of his duties
Honesty	One must be honest to his organisation/employer
Visit sick people	It is virtuous action
Good advice	Give honest and beneficial advice to your colleagues and subordinates

Support subordinates	One who supports, Allah (SWT) helps him
Selection and recruitment	All must be linked to merit
Teaching & learning	Teach good manners to your subordinates
The manager must be a role model	The prophet (ﷺ) was a complete example to follow
Managing issues	Manage issues with justice
Exemplary ethics	The manager must be an example for others
Organisation policies	All must benefit employees
Quality management	It must be the second nature of both employers and employees

8 CASE STUDY: THE TREATY OF HODHABIA

Introduction

There are several reasons for the selection of Hodhabia as a case study. First, it was the non-fighting expedition of the prophet. Secondly, he has avoided a war due to his vigilance and foresight. Thirdly, he had negotiated with Quraysh while previous encounters were armed 'meetings'. The prophet (ﷺ) had to manage his companions because of the conditions of the treaty. They were defensive in nature. And the prophet (ﷺ) was given glad tiding of 'disguised glory' in the apparent retreat. The Divine Will was with the prophet.

The story

According to Lings[1] One night towards its end he dreamed that with his head shaved he entered the

---

[1] P. 247

Ka'bah, and its key was in his hand. The next day he told his Companions of this and invited them to perform the Lesser Pilgrimage with him, whereupon they hastily set about preparing so that they could leave as soon as possible. Between them, they purchased seventy camels to be sacrificed in the sacred precinct. Their meat would then be distributed among the poor of Mecca. The Prophet (ﷺ) decided to take one of his wives with him, and when lots were cast the lot fell to Umm Salamah.

Consequently, he has announced in and around Madinah about his intention of performing Umrah. He appointed two companions as his deputy and marched towards Makkah in 6 A.H. with 1400 companions. He wore ihram and prepared animals for sacrifice at Zulhalifah (The boundary of harum from Madinah side).

He had also appointed an intelligence officer to know the possible reaction of Quraysh or other tribes. The officer informed him at Asfaan and described the plans of enemy tribes on the way to Makkah. They were getting prepared to stop the prophet (ﷺ) on the way to his destination.

The prophet (ﷺ) consulted his team and put forward two proposals: to fight with these tribes and clear the way to reach Makkah, or avoid them and continue the journey. He opted the later scheme. Meanwhile, the prophet (ﷺ) came to know that Quraysh was also in fighting 'mode' and they had dispatched a squad of 200 horse riders under the command of Khalid bin Waleed through another intelligence sources. Khalid was planning to attack while Muslims were supposed to pray salat. Allah (SWT) sent down the special order of praying in the battlefield. It restricted the enemy to take advantage of the opportunity. On top of that, the prophet (ﷺ) changed his way to avoid any more encounter with Quraysh. The path was difficult and rocky, but he continued till Hodhabia and encamped there near small water well.

Tribes of Khaza was a confederate of Muslims, some of them approached the Prophet and explained him the plans of Quraysh. Badheel bin Warqa informed him that they would never allow you to enter Makkah. The prophet (ﷺ) said they were not there to fight but if they would be forced to do so "I swear to Allah that I will fight with them for the cause of my mission until I get martyred, or they would be defeated". Nevertheless, he put a peace proposal for them. Badheel conveyed the message to Quraysh who sent their ambassador for further conversation.

Both sides exchanged their views through representatives but without outcome because Quraysh was die-heart. They sent a group of 70/80 warriors to secretly attack Muslims to damage the peace talks. Muslim guards captured them, but the prophet (ﷺ) realised them as a positive gesture to continue peace efforts.

The prophet (ﷺ) had deputed Usman (RA) to talk to Quraysh after consultation with others. He was selected because he was a respectable person of mild temperament, and his clan was still in Makkah. In case of any accident, his clan could help him out. The prophet (ﷺ) advised him:

- Tell them that we are peaceful.
- Invite them towards Islam
- Give glad tiding to the Muslim still living in Makkah about the dominance of Islam in Makkah soon.

Usman (RA) conveyed the message of the prophet (ﷺ) to the key figures of Quraysh. They offered him to do tawaf of Kaaba, but he refused. Quraysh asked him to stay a little bit more so that they could decide about the outcome of the conversation.

Meanwhile, a rumour reached the prophet (ﷺ) that Usman (RA) was got martyred. The prophet (ﷺ) reacted quickly and asked his companions to get prepare for a battle. He took famous pledge known in the Islamic history as "Bait-e- Rizwaan". It was the pledge of the fight for the cause of Allah (SWT) and remain steadfast in the battlefield. However, soon after it, Usman (RA) returned, and he took the same as well.

Quraysh got the message and immediately sent their mediator. The competing parties arrived at a truce. Some conditions were against the Muslims but other conditions provided them strength. Quraysh was forced to accept Islam as a force which compelled them to allow Muslims to do Umrah the following year.

Allah (SWT) gave glad tidings of victory to the prophet. Muslims officially included their confederate (i.e. Banu Khaza) in their ranks. Doors opened to other tribes to join hands with Muslims. The treaty offered a decade of peace for them. Peace always supports Muslim cause because it provides an opportunity for Muslims to present their message to others. War used to be a source of blood shed that increases the gulf of hatred. It creates a communication gap that hinders non-Muslims to study and understand Islam.

Muslims were under moral pressure when Abu Jandal (RA) arrived and solicit the help of the prophet. The prophet (ﷺ) tried to settle dawn his matter, but the negotiator was his father who was not ready at any cost to leave him with Muslims. The prophet (ﷺ) advised him, "he remain patient". He said to the nearest effect that Allah (SWT) would open a door of salvation for you and all those who were suffering from the hands of infidels.

Managerial Implications

The implications are based upon the key actions and decisions of the prophet (ﷺ) to manage the treaty of Hodhabia. The impact of these elements was on the four areas we have identified in the introduction of the chapter.

The trigger of the expedition was the Divine guidance which appeared in the form of a dream. Remember that Ibrahim (AS) also dreamed about the sacrifice of his son. Our prophet (ﷺ) had interpreted it i.e. that he should perform umrah. He also dreamed at the occasion of Uhad and interpreted it as it happened.

First, he disseminated information about his intention or programme to the inhabitants of Madinah and the other Muslims of the time. It implies that managers should inform everyone for any initiative the organisation wanted to take in the future. He had applied the available channels of communication, the human medium.

The prophet (ﷺ) had appointed one of his colleagues to function as a deputy to his job. He used to lead prayers and managing the day-to-day affairs of the city, in fact, the newly born state of Madinah. All managers should appoint a second-hand command whenever they are out of the station.

It is important to know the movements of opponents in the war or in marketing/business management. Management information systems is a current way to gather information. The prophet (ﷺ) had appointed an information officer to keep an eye on the activities of enemies. He received the news that some tribes on the way to Makkah were getting prepared for an armed encounter. Since the purpose of the journey did not coincide with the situation on the ground, therefore, he avoided them. The prophet (ﷺ) also kept himself away from the possible interference of Quraysh military squad. It suggests that he *focused* on his objective. Contemporary management writers believe it as a key function of a Chief Executive Officer (CEO).[1]

Nevertheless, when Badheel informed him about the intentions of Quraysh, he reiterated his intention and had shown his determination to implement/achieve his mission at any cost. His determination forced Quraysh to rethink about their plan to stop him at all costs. Consequently, they sent their envoy to commence a dialogue. It suggests the prophet (ﷺ) was guiding his followers consistently. [2]

The prophet (ﷺ) had deputed Usman (RA) for further talks. He went to Makkah and did his job. Meanwhile, a rumour circulated about the martyrdom of Usman (RA). The prophet(ﷺ) reacted immediately and took an oath from his companions for a war. It forced Quraysh to start a negotiation. The new envoy completed the peace

---

[1] Johnson, Rick (2018) The Four Primary Functions of CEO Leadership, Retrieved from http://www.groco.com/readingroom/bus_ceoleadership_functions.aspx.

[2] Experts believe a CEO "guides courses of action in operations", from "Roles and Responsibilities of Chief Executive Officer of a Corporation", Retrieved from https://managementhelp.org/chiefexecutives/job-description.htm#roles.

talks which ended at a truce. Thus, the prophet (ﷺ) had achieved his objective out of the journey.

He encountered a challenge from the companions when they did not respond about his decision to abandon umrah and return to Madinah as per the conditions of the treaty. He resolved it amicably as well. He started to conclude the umrah by shaving his head and changing the special dress. The companions followed him. Thus, he presented himself as what is called in management literature as "Role model".[1]

We can summarise his decisions as shown in table 1.

Table 1 Summary of the prophet's decisions		
Triggers	**Decision**	**Impact**
Dream/Devine order	Do umrah	Truce of Hodhabia
His movement towards Makkah	Avoid enemies	Enemies failed to stop him
Allah's command	Initiated talks	Achieved peace and

---

[1] Smith, p. 364.

(Need for a peace truce)		long-term victory
Enemy attack but Muslim army captured the invaders	Set them freed	Created positive image about Muslims
Non-compliance of companions for abandoning umrah	He started the initiative	The issue was resolved

Bibliography

Adair, John (2010) The Leadership of Muhammad (pbuh), New Delhi: Kogan Page India Private Limited.

Al-Bahaqi, Abi Bakker Ahmad Al-Hussain (2009) Dhalail Al-Nabuwwa, Karachi: Dharul Ishaat.

Allen, Louis A. (1958) Management and organization, New York: McGraw-Hill.

DeCenzo, David A. and Stephen P. Robbins (2010) Human Resource Management, New York: John Wiley & Sons.

Dess, Gregory G., G. T. Lumpkin, Alan B. Eisner (2006) Strategic Management: Text and Cases, New York: Irwin/McGraw-Hill.

Dyck, B and Mitchell J Neubert (2009) Principal of Management, South-Western.

Fulop, L, and S Linstead (1999) Management, A critical text, London: Macmillan.

Haimann, Theo and Raymond L. Hilgert (1972) Supervision: Concepts and Practices of Management, South-Western Publishing Company.

Hameed Ullah, M. (2006) The Prophet's (ﷺ) Establishing a State and his Succession, Beacon Books: Lahore.

Iqbal, Javed, and Muhammad Mushtaq Ahmad (2009) Planning in the Islamic Tradition: The Case of Hijrah Expedition, INSIGHTS 01(3), 37-68.

Kaandhlawi, Muhammad Zakarya (1997), Fazail-e-Amaal, Lahore: Kutibkhana Faizi.

Kaandhlawi, Muhammad Yusaf (2012), Hayatus Sahabah, Delhi: Islamic Books Services.

Koontz, Harold, and Heinz Weihrich (2006) Essentials of Management, New Delhi: Tata McGraw-Hill Education, pp. 81-84.

Kreitner, R (2009) Principal of Management, South-Western.

Lings, M M (1994) Muhammad, his life based on the earliest sources, Lahore: Suhail Academy.

Mubarakpuri, Safiur Rahman (1995) "The Sealed Nectar" (Ar-Raheeq Al-Makhtum), Lahore: Al-Maktba Alsalfia.

Nadvi, Sulaiman Hussaini (2205) Khutbat-e-Seerat, Karachi: Zam-Zam Publishers.

Noamani, Shibli and Syed Solaiman Nadhvi (2004) Seeratun-Nabi, Karachi: Dharul-Ishaat.

Pea, Roy D. (2015) What Is Planning Development the Development of? Accessed: April 2015, http://web.stanford.edu/~roypea/RoyPDF%20folder/A11_Pea_82d.pdf

Phalwari, Muhammad Jaafer (1995) Peghambr-e-Insaniat, Lahore: Idara Sakafat-e-Islamia.

Razi, Muhammad Wali (1987) Hadhi-e-Alam, Dharul-Ilm: Karachi.

Robbins, Stephen, and Mary Coulter (2017) Management, New Delhi: Pearson Education.

Saani, Javed Iqbal (2017) Prophet (ﷺ) Muhammad (ﷺ) as a planning expert, London: Intellectual Capital Enterprise Limited.

Saani, Javed Iqbal (2016) Responsibilities of Managers: Selected Ahadith, available on amazon.co.uk. (Paperback edition)

Siddiqi, Naeem (1997) The Benefactor of Humanity (Mohsin-e-Insaniyat), Dehli: Markazi Matabah Islami Publishers.

Smith, Mike (2007) Fundamentals of Management, Berkshire: McGraw Hill Education.

Time Management Guide (2015) What is planning and why you need to plan, Accessed: April 2015, http://www.time-management-guide.com/planning.html

Books of Ahadith

Muhammad ibn Isma`il al-Bukhari al-Ju`fi (1983) Sahih Al-Bukhari, Translated by Muhammad Muhsin Khan, Lahore: Kazi Publications.

Imâm Abut Hussain Muslim bin al-Hajjaj, SahIh Muslim, Translated by Nasiruddin al-Khattab, Riyadh, 2007, Maktaba Dar-us-Salam.

Muslim ibn al-Ḥajjāj al-Qushayrī (1971-75) Translated by Abdul Hameed Siddiqui Sahih Muslim, Lahore, Sh. Muhammad Ashraf.

Imâm Hâfiz Abu Dawud, Sunan Abu Dawud Sulaiman bin Ash'ath, Maktaba Dar-us-Salam, Riyadh, 2007.

Imäm Hãfiz Abü 'Elsa Mohammad Ibn 'Elsa At-Tirmidhi, Jamia' At-Tirm1dhi, English Translation by Abu Khaliyl, Riyadh, 2007, Maktaba Dar-us-Salam.

Imiim Hiifiz Abu Abdur Rahmiin

Ahmad bin Shu'aib bin 'Ali

An-Nasa'i, Sunan An-Nasa'i, Riyadh, 2007, Maktaba Dar-us-Salam.

Imam Muhammad Bin Yazeed

Ibn Majah Al-Qazwinf, Sunan Ibn Majah Translated by Nasiruddin al-Khattab, Riyadh, 2007, Maktaba Dar-us-Salam.

Abu Zakaria Al-Nawawi, Riyad-us-Saliheen, Riyadh, 2007, Maktaba Dar-us-Salam.

Abu Zakaria Al-Nawawi, Arbaeen Nawawi, Riyadh, 2007, Maktaba Dar-us-Salam.

Imam Malik bin Ans (RA), Muwatta Imam Malik, translated in Urdu by Allama Molana Abdul Hakeem Akhtar Shahjahanpuri, Lahore: Fareed Book Stall, accessed on 14 November 2017, https://readingpk.com/muwatta-imam-malik-imam-muhammad-malik/

https://www.sunnah.com

Index

A

Abu Musa, 12
Abyssinia, 37, 38, 41, 58
Accountability, 23, 80
Al-Bukhari, 71, 72, 73, 74
Ali, 12
Allah, Xv, 10, 70
Allah (SWT), Xvii, 1, 3, 9, 15, 16, 17, 18, 23, 25, 35, 36, 38, 40, 45, 47, 48, 55, 58, 70, 87, 91, 92, 93
Anas, Viii
Appointed, 110
Appointment, 76
Associate, 110
Australia, *111*

B

Brotherhood, 31

C

Case Study, 116
Change, 20, 42, 47, 68, 116
Chief Executive Officer, 95
Consultation, 17, 24, 59, 60, 77, 85, 91
Counsel, 60, 73
Courtesy, 72
Culture, 67

D

Day, *70*
Day Of Judgement, Xi, 58
Decision Making, 63
Decisions, 49, 57, 59, 60, 61, 62, 63, 64, 93, 96
Deputy, 90, 94

E

England, *110*

G

Greeting, 70, 77

H

Hadith, Ix, Xi, 11, 12, 22, 70, 72, 73, 74, 75, 86
Hadith Number, 11
Hereafter, 2, 3, 4, 5, 10, 11, 40
Hijrah, 36
Hiring, 25
Hodhaibia, 43
Honesty, 71, 87

I

Implications, 64, 93
Innovation, 33, 35, 36, 37
Interest, 23, 29, 37, 49, 52
Involvement, 24, 57

Iqbal, Xix
Islam, 3, 5, 9, 10, 15, 18, 21, 24, 27, 29, 34, 37, 38, 39, 44, 47, 48, 50, 52, 53, 54, 58, 62, 64, 68, 84, 85, 92, 93
Issues, 1, 43, 57, 62, 79, 81, 88

J

Jami` At-Tirmidhi, 12
Judicial System, 62
Justice, 23, 38, 54, 88

K

Kandhelvi, 4, 12, 14, 62
Knowledge, Viii, Ix, Xvii, 17, 20, 61, 62, 64, 71, 77, 111
Knowledge Management, 61

L

Leader, Xviii, 1, 16, 17, 29, 43, 45, 48, 60, 76
Leadership, Xvii, 2, 16, 17, 18, 67, 76

M

Madinah, Xviii, 5, 9, 13, 21, 30, 36, 41, 43, 44, 47, 48, 54, 58, 62, 90, 94, 96
Makkah, 2, 6, 14, 19, 21, 23, 29, 31, 34, 36, 39, 40, 41, 44, 47, 51, 54, 58, 64, 68, 90, 91, 92, 94, 95, 96
Management, 101

Management, Xvii, 8, 18, 20, 24, 63, 94, 99, 100, 101, 110, 116
Management Thoughts, 57
Managers, 115, 116
MANAGING ETHICS, 81
Messenger, 10
Migration, 5, 30, 38
Motivation, 2, 8, 10, 16, 40
Mubarikpuri, 1, 15, 19, 61
Muhammad, Vii, X, 14, 19, 23, 39, 42, 99, 100, 101, 115, 116
Muslim, 70
Muslim Manager, 18, 24, 54
Muslims, 8, 12, 14, 17, 24, 37, 38, 43, 44, 45, 46, 47, 48, 51, 55, 64, 73, 83, 85, 91, 92, 93, 94, 97
Mutual Respect, 69

O

Organisation, Xvii, Xviii, 16, 30, 52, 63, 68, 77, 84, 86, 87, 94
Organisational Culture, 68
Organizations, 27

P

Partnership, 31, 35, 37, 50, 52

Performance, 11, 17, 53, 76, 85
Plan, 101
POLICIES, 83
Polytheism, 36, 49
Prophet, 10, 115
Prophet (ﷺ), Xvii, Xviii, 1, 2, 3, 5, 7, 8, 9, 10, 11, 12, 15, 16, 17, 18, 20, 21, 22, 23, 28, 29, 30, 31, 32, 34, 35, 36, 37, 41, 42, 43, 44, 45, 46, 47, 48, 49, 51, 54, 57, 58, 59, 60, 61, 62, 63, 64, 68, 71, 76, 77, 78, 79, 80, 81, 82, 84, 85, 86

Q

Quraysh, 5, 14, 37, 47, 57, 59, 89, 90, 91, 92, 95

R

Relationship, 20, 21, 22
Remuneration, 9, 24, 28, 54
Resources, 54
Responsibility, 5, 9, 23, 28, 51
Role Model, 22, 88
ROLE MODEL, 78

S

Salaries, 27
Selection And Recruitment, 75, 87
Sick, 11, 12, 71, 87
Society, 27, 30, 38, 49, 50, 55, 84
Strategy, 2, 8, 10, 11, 12, 16, 21, 35, 36, 40, 42, 44, 45, 46, 47, 61

T

Taif, 39, 58, 63, 64, 80
Thuwair, 12
Tolerant, 3
Training, 16, 35, 78
Trigger, 69, 94

V

Values, 31, 84, 86, 87
  Punctuality, 84, 85
Values
  Quality, 85, 86

W

Wealth, 33, 37, 49, 50, 52, 54

Z

Zakat, 50, 51, 73
Zulhalifah, 90

Other books by the author (s)

1. Prof Dr. Javed Iqbal Saani (2018) Leading Strategy of the Prophet (ﷺ), Intellectual Capital Enterprise Limited, London, available on amazon (Paperback edition)
2. Prof Dr. Javed Iqbal Saani (2018) Organising Strategy of the Prophet (ﷺ), Intellectual Capital Enterprise Limited, London, available on amazon (Paperback edition)
3. Prof Dr. Javed Iqbal Saani (2018) Planning Strategy of the Prophet (ﷺ), Intellectual Capital Enterprise Limited, London, available on amazon (Paperback edition)
4. Prof Dr. Javed Iqbal Saani (2018) Qualities of Momins: The Quranic Perspective, Intellectual Capital Enterprise Limited, London, available on amazon (Paperback edition)
5. Prof Dr. Javed Iqbal Saani (2018) Hajj Experience: Combining Dawah and Manasiks, Intellectual Capital Enterprise Limited, London, available on amazon (Paperback edition)

6. Prof Dr. Javed Iqbal Saani (2018) Sukhn-e-Saani (The book of poetry), Intellectual Capital Enterprise Limited, London, available on amazon (Paperback edition)
7. Prof Dr. Javed Iqbal Saani (2018) Managing Your Projects, Intellectual Capital Enterprise Limited, London, available on amazon.co.uk. (Paperback edition)
8. Prof Dr. Javed Iqbal Saani (2017) Business Case Studies, Intellectual Capital Enterprise Limited, London, available on amazon (Paperback edition)
9. Prof Dr. Javed Iqbal Saani (2017) Virtues of Sickness: Selected Ahadith, available on amazon (Paperback edition)
10. Prof Dr. Javed Iqbal Saani (2017) Prophet (ﷺ) Muhammad (ﷺ) as a planning expert, available on amazon (Paperback edition)
11. Prof Dr. Javed Iqbal Saani (2017) Muhammad (ﷺ): His Trials & Tribulations, available on amazon (Paperback edition)
12. Prof Dr. Javed Iqbal Saani (2017) Sales and Marketing: Selected Ahadith, available on amazon.co.uk. (Paperback edition)
13. Prof Dr. Javed Iqbal Saani (2016) Research Proposals: Contents & Exemplars, available on amazon.co.uk. (Paperback edition)

14. Prof Dr. Javed Iqbal Saani (2016) Responsibilities of Managers: Selected Ahadith, available on amazon.co.uk. (Paperback edition)
15. Prof Dr. Javed Iqbal Saani (2016) Experience: The Journey of My Life, available on amazon.co.uk. (Paperback edition)
16. Prof Dr. Javed Iqbal Saani (2012) Understanding Information Systems, Manchester: GRaASS.
17. Prof Dr Javed Iqbal Saani (2011) Digital Divide in South Asia ISBN: 9789699578120.
18. Prof Dr. Javed Iqbal Saani and Muhammad Rafi Khattak (2011) Managing Risk in Projects, ISBN: 9789699578090.
19. Prof Dr. Javed Iqbal Saani and Muhammad Nadeem Khan (2011, 2018) Understanding Project Management, ISBN: 978969957845, available on amazon (Paperback edition)
20. Prof Dr. Javed Iqbal Saani (2011) Information Systems for Managers, Grass Books, Manchester.
21. Prof Dr. Javed Iqbal Saani (2010) Managing strategic change: a real-world case study, ISBN: 978-3838330952, available on amazon.co.uk. (Paperback edition)

[Please see the images of these books on the following pages in addition to my doctoral thesis]

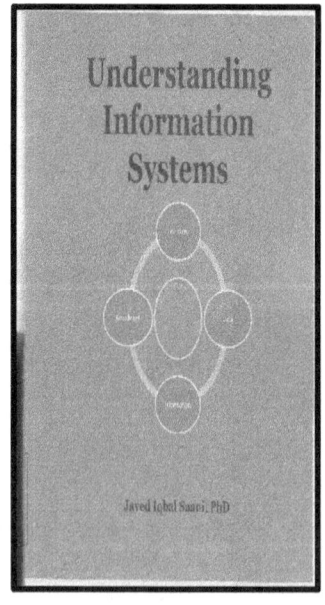

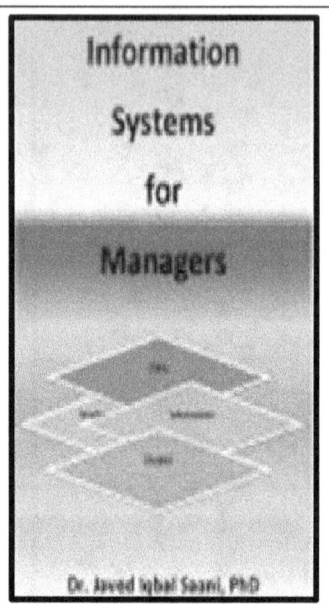

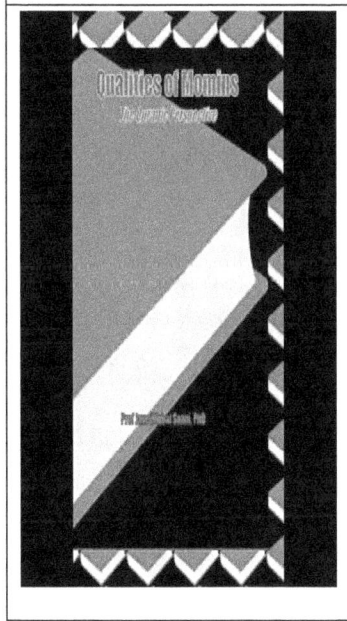

Notes

www.ingramcontent.com/pod-product-compliance
Lightning Source LLC
Chambersburg PA
CBHW071551220526
45469CB00003B/981